CAF

The D

2022 Long W

Andrew Delaplaine

NO BUSINESS HAS PAID A SINGLE PENNY OR GIVEN _ANYTHING_ TO BE INCLUDED IN THIS BOOK.

Senior Writer **- James Cubby**

Gramercy Park Press
New York – London – Paris

CAPE COD
The Delaplaine
Long Weekend Guide

TABLE OF CONTENTS

Chapter 1
WHY CAPE COD?

Every time I'm in the Hamptons, the thought crosses my mind that "I'd rather be on Cape Cod."

Every time I'm on Cape Cod, I think two things: "Thank God it never turned into the Hamptons" and "Thank God it's still the same."

It's not of course. Nothing ever really is the same. But when you run into old-timers on Long Island, they'll tell you how it was in the Hamptons before the mega-rich moved in and built their monstrously inappropriate mansions, bringing along with them, naturally, their monstrously inappropriate attitudes. The Hamptons with their fancy shops and nightclubs. (Can you ever imagine a NIGHTCLUB on Cape Cod? Not really. Who would ever go to it?

I'm not including P-town in this statement—with all the gay people out there, of course they have nightclubs.)

Cape Cod is really one of the great things about America. There's a unique ecosystem or lifestyle or way of life or mindset on the Cape, however you may want to describe it.

The cheesy little stores selling dust collecting souvenirs, the roadside seafood shacks selling fried clams the way they have for decades, the quiet beaches on Nantucket Bay, the shops selling saltwater taffy and other summer goodies—all of it is remarkably the same as it was when my grandmother used to drag us out there from Boston every summer.

It's kinda like the northern version of the Florida Keys. (Though the local people couldn't be more different if they tried—the ones up on the Cape actually read books and know who's President. In the Keys, they couldn't care less.)

Like Key West, Cape Cod, and especially P-town, has been a magnate for artists of every type. If you're lucky, you might be able to catch filmmaker John Waters tooling around town on his weird looking bike.

Just as the Keys are divided into three parts, the Upper, Middle and Lower Keys, Cape Cod goes them one better and is divided roughly into four parts: the Upper Cape, Mid-Cape, Lower Cape and Outer Cape. (Five parts if you count the Islands—Martha's Vineyard, Nantucket and Gosnold.)

UPPER CAPE
The Upper Cape runs north to south and is bounded by Buzzards Bay and the Cape Cod Canal. Sandwich takes the honors as the oldest town on the Cape, thus the most historic. Charming Falmouth and its lovely waterfront aren't far away. Wood's Hole, of course, is home to the big oceanographic institute you've probably heard a lot about over the years. Then there's Mashpee, New Seabury, Bourne.

MID-CAPE
Exactly as the name indicates, Mid-Cape is in the middle of the peninsula, boasting towns like Hyannis (famed for its Kennedy connection), Osterville (where we stayed with grandmother in a whitewashed house), Barnstable Village, Dennis, Yarmouthport, Centerville, West Barnstable, Craigville, Cummaquid, HyannisPort.

LOWER CAPE

In the geography of the "arm" that Cape Cod forms, this area starts at the elbow and makes its way north. Chatham is the jewel of the Lower Cape, sporting a charmingly quaint downtown area, shops and restaurants. Chatham makes a great place to stay because it's so centrally located to the rest of Cape Cod. Here you'll find Also in the Lower Cape is Orleans, claimed to be the spot where Leif Eriksson landed in 1003. (Long before the lobster roll, he probably had his lobster cooked over a spit with no drawn butter and loved them just as much as we do today.) Also here you'll find Harwichport and Brewster.

The thing that gets me about Leif Eriksson is why in God's name he didn't send his boat back and tell the crew to bring their families. Think of the real estate he could have stolen from the Indians.

OUTER CAPE

As the "forearm" of Cape Cod moves north, you enter what is called the Outer Cape. On one side you have Cape Cod Bay and on the other the Atlantic. The peninsula becomes quite narrow out here, and you pass through towns like Eastham (not that there's much of a "town" there) and Truro with great views from the cliffs and the Cape Cod Light, before you get to wonderful Wellfleet. (Think "Wellfleet oysters.") This is a great little town I love very much, a civilized respite from the madness of the last stop,

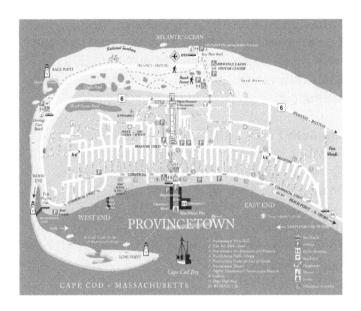

Provincetown, or "P-town" to locals, a sizeable
number of whom are gay.
P-town is a world unto its own on Cape Cod. There
are dozens of little towns on the Cape you could pick
up, move 20 or 30 miles and set down again and
nobody would notice anything different. But you
couldn't do that with P-town. It's completely unique.

THE ISLANDS
Martha's Vineyard & Nantucket
Several Cape Cod harbors have ferries that will take
you to Martha's Vineyard.
The **Island Queen** operates out of Falmouth Harbor.
Quickest way if you don't have a car. 30-40 minutes
from dock to dock. 75 Falmouth Heights Rd, 508-
548-4800. www.islandqueen.com/

Steamship Authority takes cars over. Must reserve a place for your car. 1 Cowdry Rd, Wood's Hole, and also from 65 South St, Hyannis. 508-495-3278 for people reservations, 508-477-8600 to reserve a place for your car. www.steamshipauthority.com/

Falmouth Ferry , 278 Scranton Ave, Falmouth, 508-548-9400. www.falmouthedgartownferry.com/ Offers only service to Edgartown in the summer aboard a 72-foot vessel.

Hy-Line Cruises
220 Ocean St, Hyannis, 508-778-2600
hylinecruises.com/
Serves both islands.

WHEN TO VISIT
I prefer the slightly off-season Spring and Autumn periods over the high summer season to visit Cape Cod. But then, I can do without most beach activities that if you have a family, you'll want to take advantage of. Kids want to swim. The worst time for me is 4th of July through Labor Day. This is the high summer season. The four weeks before or the four weeks after make the perfect time to visit. The crowds are less, the rates are lower, you can get into the best restaurants without a hassle and the car traffic is reduced to somewhat sane levels, not something you can say in high season.

Chapter 2
GETTING ABOUT

You will need a car, pure and simple.
There is bus service along the Cape. Details at
www.p-b.com. But once you get into a town, you'll
be at the mercy of taxis, which can be expensive,
even for short jaunts.
In 2013, a new train service was started (the first
since 1959), called the **Cape Flyer**.
www.capeflyer.com -- it's a weekend service that
runs from Boston's South Street Station Friday-

Sunday Memorial Day through Labor Day. Definitely worth checking out if you're going to a certain location and don't plan to travel around the Cape very much.

Chapter 3
WHERE TO STAY

Bungalows

An old song has this lyric: "In a cozy bungalow, we'd know such sweet delight." From one end of the Cape to the other you'll find hundreds of these bungalows, cottages, what-have-you. While they are quaint and look great, if you want the bungalow experience, be sure you choose carefully. Once you go into some of these little houses, you see how awful so many of them can be. Another thing: lots of places are not open all year.

21 BROAD
21 Broad St, Nantucket, 508-228-4749
www.21broadhotel.com
Located in Nantucket's most popular historic neighborhood, this Urban-style boutique hotel (carved out of a 27-room Victorian mansion) offers an ideal setting for a relaxed getaway. This unique hotel offers 27 modern rooms with comfortable bedding and blackout shades for late-sleepers. Amenities include: Vitamin C showers, guest lounge with game table, outdoor courtyard, LED Smart TVs, complimentary wireless internet, breakfast and daily housekeeping. On-site spa.

ASHLEY MANOR
3660 Main St, Barnstable, 508-362-8044
www.ashleymanor.net
Originally built in 1699, this romantic bed & breakfast is located in the heart of the historic district with six beautifully appointed guest rooms – four are suites with wood-burning fireplaces, two-person Jacuzzi tub, and complimentary Wi-Fi. Conveniently located near Cape Cod Bay, Barnstable Village and Barnstable Harbor. Complimentary breakfast in the morning and cordials at night.

BELFRY INNE & BISTRO
6 Jarves St, Sandwich, 508-888-8550
www.belfryinn.com
There certainly is a lot of history here. This B&B is
spread out over 3 historic buildings: a Victorian home
from 1872 called the Painted Lady, a disused Catholic
church (the Abbey) and an 1830 Federal style
building now called the Village House. Very
charming, everything about this place. Each room is
entirely different from the others. Spa services. The
Belfry Bistro serves dinner Tuesday-Sunday: Sirloin
Carpaccio, asparagus bisque; baked stuffed
littlenecks; lavender poached codfish; bacon-wrapped
pork tenderloin. Lunch is served next door at newly
opened Burger Bar.

BRASS KEY GUESTHOUSE
67 Bradford St, Provincetown, 508-276-7166
www.brasskey.com

Across the street and down a bit from the **Crown Pointe** is this little upmarket complex of 9 restored historic buildings, a pool and gardens. Some rooms have fireplaces and whirlpools. Nice bar, the **Shipwreck Lounge**, where I've found myself wrecked a few times too many. On-site Spa as well. Lively crowd (mostly gay).

CANDLEBERRY INN
1882 Main St, Brewster, 508-896-3300
www.candleberryinn.com
Located in the Old Kings Highway Historic District, this historic inn offers beautifully decorated rooms. Amenities include: complimentary Wi-Fi and newspapers, complimentary full breakfast, and flat screen TVs. Conveniently located near activities like biking, whaling, shopping, fishing, golfing, kayaking, and shopping. A smoke-free bed & breakfast venue.

CAPTAIN'S HOUSE INN
369 Old Harbor Rd, Chatham, 508-945-0127
www.captainshouseinn.com
It really was a captain's cottage. Now this luxurious B&B is quite a bit more: you can choose to stay in a **Greek Revival mansion** dating from 1839; a **Carriage House** with 5 lovely rooms converted from an old barn; **the Stables** originally were a tool shed and then a bunkhouse for interns—now it houses 3 of the nicest rooms in the whole property; the **Captain's Cottage** has 3 rooms, each quite nice. A very good breakfast is served from 8-10, but here they also offer you afternoon tea from 3-5 and snacks from 6:30 to 10:30. Free port and sherry in the library.

CHATHAM BARS INN
297 Shore Rd, Chatham, 800-527-4884
www.chathambarsinn.com
This stately property opened up in 1914 and conveys
a palpable sense of what "old Cape Cod" was really
like. Conde Nast rates it among the top properties in
the area. You can choose to stay in the Main Inn, the
Cottage Rooms or take a Spa Suite and enjoy all the
spa services available here. Afternoon tea. Lots of
dining options, too: **Stars** offers up New England
cuisine in a plush setting overlooking the ocean; the
Tavern is where you'll want to hang out for a drink
and maybe eat, much more laid back than Stars; the
Beach House Grill is outside and great in the
summer. They even have a 55-foot Hinckley to take

you to Martha's Vineyard or Nantucket. Every base is covered here.

THE CHEQUIT
23 Grand Ave, Shelter Island Heights, Shelter Island, 631-749-0018
www.thechequithotel.com/
Formerly The Salt House Inn, this newly reopened hotel offers 31 rooms and a six-bedroom cottage all decorated in shabby-chic but offering a luxurious experience.

COLONY OF WELLFLEET
640 Chequessett Neck Rd, Wellfleet, 508-349-3761
www.colonyofwellfleet.com
The group of cottages (dating from 1948) overlooking Wellfleet Harbor and bay was originally built as a private club and art gallery. The Stefanis took over in

1963, and have really made the place their own. They offer six 1-bedroom and four 2-bedroom cottages. Cash or check only. No credit cards. 50% deposit required.

COTTAGE GROVE
1975 State Hwy, Eastham, 877-521-5522
www.grovecape.com
Knotty-pine cottages spread out over 3 acres densely forested with pines, oaks, low-slung shrubbery. Takes pets. May-Oct. For the real rustic experience, this is the place.

COTTAGES AT MAUSHOP VILLAGE
In Mashpee
Properties managed by Mercantile Property Management
18 Waterhouse, Buzzards Bay, 508-759-5555
www.mercantileproperty.com/maushopvillage/home.asp
 The cottages here are newer, and it's really a condo development made up of cottages that individual owners lease to people like you. The website has a list of currently available cottages. Follow up from there. Right on the beach.

THE COVE
183 Main St, West Yarmouth, 508-771-3666
www.coveatyarmouth.com
This is a big resort, with over 200 suites and townhouses. Each lodging has separate bedroom and living room areas, wet bar, refrigerator, stereo, two LCD color televisions, a DVD Player, coffee maker,

microwave and toaster. Large indoor and outdoor pools, fully equipped fitness facility, racquetball, volleyball or indoor and outdoor tennis courts. There's a spa here as well. The on-site restaurant is very ordinary, so plan on taking your meals at any of the excellent restaurants nearby. Or use their BBQ area and do your own cookouts.

THE COVE MOTEL
13 S Orleans Rd, Orleans, 508-255-1203
www.thecoveorleans.com
Perfect place that's close to Hyannis, but away from all the crowds, making it the perfect romantic hideaway. Looks a little underwhelming but when you get inside you'll see that it's one of the best value places to stay in the area. Has only 40 units, different sizes, from single rooms to 2-bedroom suites. Has a superior view of the Orleans cove and a pool that overlooks the cove as well.

CROWNE POINTE
82 Bradford St, Provincetown, 508-413-6747
www.crownepointe.com
Across the street and down a bit from the **BRASS KEY GUESTHOUSE** is this complex centered around a 19th Century house featuring pool and gardens. You've got 6 historic buildings here lovingly restored. Can't get a better location in P-town. Hardwood floors, tasteful décor. Afternoon tea as well as free wine and cheese prior to dinner. Their restaurant is **The Pointe**, an intimate place (only 50 seats) in the old captain's mansion. Menu highlights: locally caught fish, bacon & deviled eggs, poached lobster & chive gnocchi, tuna tartare & caviar. On site **Shui Spa** is full-service. No kids under 16 (this is a romantic getaway, remember?), but they have one room that they'll let pets stay in.

CROW'S NEST RESORT
496 Shore Rd, North Truro, 508-487-9031
www.caperesort.com
Motel property right across from the beach.
Reasonable.

EBEN HOUSE
90 Bradford St, Provincetown, 508-487-0386
www.ebenhouse.com
Located in the heart of Provincetown, this bed &
breakfast features a rooftop terrace and smoke-free
experience. Amenities include: complimentary full
breakfast, complimentary Wi-Fi in public areas, LCD
TVs, and premium bedding.

INN ON THE SOUND
313 Grand Ave, Falmouth, 508-457-9666
www.innonthesound.com
This lovely B&B is up 45 feet on a bluff with great
views of the ocean. You can even see Martha's
Vineyard from here. They have 10 very nice, modern
rooms. One good thing about this place: it's open all
year.

LITTLE INN ON PLEASANT BAY
654 S Orleans Rd, Orleans, 508-255-0780
www.alittleinnonpleasantbay.com
Located right in the "elbow" of the Cape you'll find
this charming B&B. Great views of the water, a small
beach, dock for fishing or swimming. They have 9
bedrooms, each individually decorated. Lots of comfy
slipcovered chairs in the public rooms. The main
house dates back to 1798. This place feels like home.
You could move right in.

OCEAN EDGE RESORT & CLUB
2907 Main Street, Brewster, 800-343-6074 or 508-
896-9000
oceanedge.com
This is quite the place. This fine mansion went up in
1912, owned by one of the town's richest families.

Now it has 300+ rooms. There are individual villas available, either on the water or facing the golf course designed by Jack Nicklaus.

THE RED INN
15 Commercial St, Provincetown, 508-487-7334
www.theredinn.com
Right on Provincetown Harbor you'll find excellent lodgings in an inn that's been here since 1915. Tasteful décor, fireplaces, beamed ceilings, wide-planked pine flooring. They have 3 nicely appointed guest rooms, 3 large suites and 2 luxury residences, all with drop-dead views of the harbor and bay. The restaurant here is also good: pan roasted local cod on a bed of rosemary potatoes and applewood bacon. The lamb chops are tops as well. The bar here makes a great place to grab a drink and absorb the atmosphere, or even better, enjoy the sunset.

SURFSIDE HOTEL & SUITES

543 Commercial St, Provincetown, 508-487-1726
www.surfsideinn.cc
April – October.
All the bright and airy rooms here are equipped with microwave, refrigerator, premium cable TV, balcony and cozy bathrobes. One- and two-bedroom apartments come with full kitchen, dining area, and living room, making them the perfect lodging choice for families. Their new first-floor waterfront suites offer Jacuzzi tubs, living room, dining area, efficiency kitchen, and private bedroom. Free Continental breakfast that's actually heads and shoulders above the others you've had. Heated saltwater pool.

WEQUASSETT RESORT & GOLF CLUB

2173 Rte 28, East Harwich, 508-432-5400
www.wequassett.com
No question this is one of the top places to stay on the Cape. Though they offer 120 rooms, they're broken up into whitewashed buildings and tidy clapboard cottages spread out over 27 acres of gardens and salt marshes. A wonderful natural setting. Also 2 pools, 4 restaurants, boating and water sports—it's all here. There are 22 buildings making up the resort, and some of them have a little history. Just to start things off and get you in the mood, all guests register in a 1740 building before going to their lodgings.

WHALEWALK INN & SPA

220 Bridge Rd, Eastham, 508-255-0617
www.whalewalkinn.com
You'll be seduced by all the antiques filling the public rooms and bedrooms in this super B&B. The inn was built in 1830 for a whaling captain, and has been used as many things since then. Converted to an inn in 1953, it's been beautifully restored and looked after. Choose to stay in the **Main Inn**, one of the **Barn Suites**, or rooms in the **Guest House**, **Carriage House** or the **Salt Box Cottage**. There's a suite called the Penthouse, with stairs going up the side of the building, that's very romantic.

WINGS NECK LIGHTHOUSE

Pocasset, MA 617-899-5063
www.wingsnecklighthouse.org
Once run by the Coast Guard to protect boats navigating the area. The lighthouse still stands. The property was auctioned off in the 1940s, and now you

can stay in the keeper's cottage. Cottage sleeps 8 people. Three upstairs bedrooms and a pullout queen sofa in the family room. Lots of amenities.

Chapter 4
WHERE TO EAT

28 ATLANTIC
2173 Massachusetts 28, East Harwick, 508-430-3000
www.wequassett.com/dining#/twenty-eight/
CUISINE: Seafood/American
DRINKS: Full Bar
SERVING: Breakfast & Dinner; open Fri, Sat & Sun
PRICE RANGE: $$$
This elegant waterfront eatery offers an impressive
menu of seafood and classic American dishes. The
eight-foot windows offer beautiful views of Pleasant
Bay.
Note: Dress code forbids denim, collarless shirts,
shorts and athletic shoes.

99
1600 Falmouth Rd, Bell Tower Mall, Centerville,
508-790-8995
14 Berry Ave, West Yarmouth, 508-862-9990
www.99restaurants.com
CUISINE: American
DRINKS: Full bar
SERVING: Lunch & Dinner daily

PRICE RANGE: $$
If you have a bunch of kids, this is the place to bring them. Reasonable prices and good-sized portions. Everything from entree salads, burgers, sandwiches and wraps, steaks and ribs, seafood, chicken and turkey, soups and sides.

400 EAST
1421 Orleans Rd #21, Harwich, 508-432-1800
www.the400east.com
CUISINE: American/Italian
DRINKS: Full Bar
SERVING: Lunch, Dinner
PRICE RANGE: $$
This casual tavern offers a menu of American comfort food. Menu favorites include thin crust pizza and fresh ground burgers.

ABBA
89 Old Colony Way, Orleans, 508-255-8144
www.abbarestaurant.com
CUISINE: Mediterranean
DRINKS: Full Bar
SERVING: Dinner
PRICE RANGE: $$$
Chef Erez Pinhas hails from Israel, and while he offers some items that reflect this (like falafel in a tahini-amba sauce), it's the Asian influences that produce standout dishes (like the shrimp & lobster pad Thai). This is not a big place, so be prepared to grab a seat at the bar if you have to. The food's worth

it. (Lots of people say this is the best restaurant on the whole Cape, but them there is fightin' words.)

ALBERTO'S RESTAURANT
360 Main St, Hyannis, 508-778-1770
www.albertos.net
CUISINE: Italian
DRINKS: Full Bar
SERVING: Lunch, Dinner
PRICE RANGE: $$$
This tried-and-true fine-dining eatery offers a menu of Northern Italian fare. Menu favorites include: Short ribs and Chicken Scaloppini with artichoke hearts. Impressive wine list.

AMARI BAR AND RESTAURANT
674 Route 6A, East Sandwich, 508-375-0011
www.amarirestaurant.com
CUISINE: Italian

DRINKS: Full Bar
SERVING: Lunch, Dinner
PRICE RANGE: $$
This welcoming bar and restaurant offers a menu of
Italian classics. Menu favorites include: Lobster and
seafood over rice, and Broiled Salmon. Live music.

ANEJO MEXICAN BISTRO & TEQUILA BAR
188 Main St, Falmouth, 508-388-7631
www.anejomexicanbistro.com
CUISINE: Mexican
DRINKS: Full Bar
SERVING: Lunch, Dinner
PRICE RANGE: $$
This contemporary Mexican eatery offers an ever-
changing menu of Tex-Mex favorites and Mexican-
style street food. Casual dining on the patio is nice
during warmer months. Reservations recommended.

ARNOLD'S LOBSTER & CLAM BAR
3580 State Hwy, Eastham, 508-255-2575

www.arnoldsrestaurant.com
CUISINE: Seafood, Ice cream and frozen yogurt
DRINKS: Full Bar
SERVING: 11:30 am – 9:30pm daily
PRICE RANGE: $$
Since 1976 they've been serving a fried lobster tail
that consistently draws raves.

BARLEY NECK INN
5 Beach Rd, Orleans, 508-255-0212
www.barleyneck.com
CUISINE: Seafood/American
DRINKS: Full Bar
SERVING: Lunch, Dinner
PRICE RANGE: $$$
Located in a historic sea captain's house, this eatery
offers four elegant rooms of dining. Favorites include:
Lobster chili and Seared Tuna. Great selection of
single malt scotches.

BAXTER'S BOATHOUSE

177 Pleasant St, Hyannis, 508-775-4490
www.baxterscapecod.com
CUISINE: Seafood
DRINKS: Full Bar
SERVING: Lunch, Dinner
PRICE RANGE: $$
Located in a boathouse built over the water, this
restaurant offers a great selection of seafood.
Favorites include the clam chowder and the fresh
haddock.

BEACH GRILL AT CHATHAM BARS INN

297 Shore Rd, Chatham, 508-945-0096
www.chathambarsinn.com
CUISINE: American/Seafood
DRINKS: Full Bar
SERVING: Lunch, Dinner

PRICE RANGE: $$$
Located on the water's edge, this is a favorite spot of local's and tourists. This venue offers an impressive menu of New England fare and panoramic view of the Atlantic and Chatham Harbor. Tasty lobster rolls and signature cocktails.

BETSY'S DINER
457 Main St, Falmouth 508-540-0060
https://betsys-diner.business.site
CUISINE: American
DRINKS: No Booze
SERVING: Lunch, Dinner
PRICE RANGE: $
This little retro eatery offers typical American diner fare from meatloaf to breakfast served all day.

BLACKFISH
17 Truro Center Rd, Truro 508-349-3399
www.blackfishtruro.com
CUISINE: American
DRINKS: Full Bar
SERVING: Lunch, Dinner
PRICE RANGE: $$$
Located in a former blacksmith shop, this eatery offers delicious seafood dishes and a bustling bar scene. Favorites include: The Bone-in Rib eye steak with truffle butter. Nice selection of wines.

BLEU
Mashpee Commons, 10 Market St, Mashpee, 508-539-7907
www.bleurestaurant.com

CUISINE: French
DRINKS: Full Bar
SERVING: Lunch, Dinner
PRICE RANGE: $$
This French eatery offers a fine dining experience with a menu of French bistro classics. Favorites include Salmon over asparagus and sweet potatoes. Nice wine pairings.

BOBBY BYRNE'S RESTAURANT & PUB
Rt 6 A Tupper Rd, Sandwich, 508-888-6088
www.bobbybyrnes.com
CUISINE: American
DRINKS: Full Bar
SERVING: Lunch, Dinner
PRICE RANGE: $$
This popular eatery offers a diverse and ample menu of homemade Pub favorites, Mexican fare, burgers, sandwiches and hearty salads. Nice wine selection. This place offers a comfortable dining experience.

BOG PUB
618 MacArthur Blvd, Pocasset 508-392-9620
www.thebogtavern.com/
CUISINE: American/Burgers
DRINKS: Full Bar
SERVING: Dinner; closed Mon
PRICE RANGE: $$
This place has a loyal following and one visit will make you a fan. The food is great. They start your dining experience with fresh warm toasted bread and flavored oil. Favorites include the clam chowder and hummus. Great bar selection.

BOOKSTORE & RESTAURANT
50 Kendrick Ave, Wellfleet 508-349-3154
www.wellfleetoyster.com
CUISINE: Seafood
DRINKS: Full Bar
SERVING: Lunch, Dinner
PRICE RANGE: $$
This popular eatery offers a great menu of tasty
seafood favorites. Great creative cocktail menu.

BRAX LANDING RESTAURANT
705 Route 28, Harwich Port, 508-432-5515
www.braxrestaurant.com
CUISINE: Seafood
DRINKS: Full Bar
SERVING: Lunch, Dinner
PRICE RANGE: $$
This popular seafood eatery offers a varied menu
including specials like the French Dip sandwich and
an impressive wine list. This is also a great choice for
Sunday Brunch with classic favorites like Eggs
Benny and a delicious selection of desserts.

BRAZILIAN GRILL
680 Main St, Hyannis Port, 508-771-0109
www.braziliangrill-capecod.com
CUISINE: Steakhouse
DRINKS: Full Bar
SERVING: Lunch, Dinner
PRICE RANGE: $$$
This steakhouse offers great all-you-can-eat specials
with a salad bar and buffet.

All-you-can-eat churrascaria serves slow-cooked meats carved tableside, with a salad bar & buffet. Great desserts.

BREWSTER FISH HOUSE
2208 Main St, Brewster, 508-896-7867
www.brewsterfishhouse.com
CUISINE: Seafood
DRINKS: Full Bar
SERVING: Lunch & dinner; NO RESERVATIONS
PRICE RANGE: $$$
Roasted bone marrow or artisanal meat & cheese platters make a good appetizer here. Seared cod, pan-roasted halibut are good main courses. Also the grilled tenderloin & scallops make a good surf & turf selection (served with a goat cheese potato puree, morels, smoked bacon, spring garlic & Béarnaise). The small cottage is quaint, but note they don't take reservations. (Like the locals, I try to swing by during lunch and skip dinner: easier to get a table.)

BRITISH BEER COMPANY
46 Rte 6-A, Sandwich, 508-833-9590
263 Grand Ave, Falmouth, 508-540-9600
412 Main St, Hyannis, 508-771-1776
www.britishbeer.com
CUISINE: American
DRINKS: Full bar
SERVING: Lunch & dinner daily
PRICE RANGE: $$
This is a chain of British style pubs serving a good selection of domestic and international craft beers, as well as a dauntingly large menu serving everything

from soups to salads to main courses. It's like most chains that put out those menus so big that you're bound to find something on it. But each location has its own friendly appeal. Dark woods, lively crowds, good pub fare, and there's music later in the evenings.

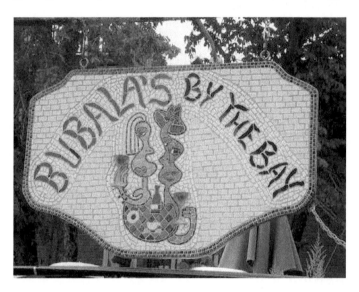

BUBALA'S BY THE BAY
185 Commercial St, Provincetown 508-487-0773
www.bubalas.com
CUISINE: American
DRINKS: Full Bar
SERVING: Lunch, Dinner
PRICE RANGE: $$
This place is known as having the best fried scallops in Provincetown. This is a great place for people watching and casual dining. Favorites include: Grilled Free-Range Chicken Breast and Lobster & Soul Roulade. Live entertainment.

BUCA'S TUSCAN ROADHOUSE
4 Depot Rd, Harwich, 508-432-6900
www.thebogtavern.com/
CUISINE: Italian
DRINKS: Full Bar
SERVING: Dinner daily from 5
PRICE RANGE: $$$
Starters like grilled goat cheese polenta topped with orange fig compote, mussels with garlic & fennel, pan-fried gnocchi. For a main course, go for the Caccuicco (littleneck clams, mussels, calamari, shrimp and catch of the day in a rich tomato sauce). They have other hearty Italian dishes like roasted chicken and garlic, eggplant parm, etc.

BUCATINO
7 Nathan Ellis Hwy, North Falmouth, 508-566-8960
www.bucawinebar.com
CUISINE: Italian
DRINKS: Full bar
SERVING: Lunch & Dinner
PRICE RANGE: $$$
Popular Italian eatery focusing on fresh seafood. The fireplace adds a lot of coziness to the atmosphere in this charming eatery. Menu picks: Bucatini Bolognese and Shrimp Ravioli. Large portions. Big bar. Excellent wine list.

C SALT WINE BAR & GRILLE
75 Davis Straits, Falmouth (774) 763-2954
www.csaltfalmouth.com
CUISINE: American/French

DRINKS: Full Bar
SERVING: Dinner; closed Tues
PRICE RANGE: $$#
Chef/owner Jonathan Philips welcomes guests to his casual bar and grill. Favorites include: Statler Chicken Breast and Grilled Petite Filet Mignon. Great wine and food pairings from an extensive wine list.

CAFÉ CHEW
4 Merchant's Rd, Sandwich 508-888-7717
www.cafechew.com
CUISINE: American
DRINKS: No Booze
SERVING: Breakfast, Brunch & Lunch
PRICE RANGE: $
Friendly café with a menu of American favorites. Popular place for breakfast and lunch with outdoor seating. Favorites include the California BLT with egg. Children's menu.

CAFÉ RIVERVIEW
451 Rt 6A, Sandwich, 508-833-8365
www.riverviewschool.org
CUISINE: American (Traditional)
DRINKS: No Booze
SERVING: Breakfast/Lunch
PRICE RANGE: $
NEIGHBORHOOD: Sandwich
Small cafe with walk up service counter serving American fare with twists like the Asian Chicken wrap. Homemade soups, quiche, and smoothies.

THE CANTEEN

225 Commercial St, Provincetown, 508-487-3800
www.thecanteenptown.com
CUISINE: Seafood/Fish & Chips
DRINKS: Beer & Wine Only
SERVING: Lunch, Dinner; closed Mon, Tues, &
Wed
PRICE RANGE: $$
A popular eatery of locals and tourists features a great
menu of seafood and sandwiches. Favorites include
Oyster po'boy sandwich and Clam chowder.

CAPE SEA GRILLE

31 Sea Street, Harwich Port, 508-432-4745
www.capeseagrille.com
CUISINE: New American
DRINKS: Full Bar
SERVING: Dinner nightly from 5; bar opens at 4:30.
PRICE RANGE: $$$
Asparagus bisque with salmon; shrimp & pork belly
ravioli topped with braised cabbage; duck confit;
local oysters on the half shell all make good starters.
My favorite entrée here is the pan seared whole
lobster with pancetta, grilled asparagus and potatoes.
Also the trio of Long Island duck (seared breast,
confit leg & seared foie gras with dried cherry sauce).
Located in a ramshackle old house, this is the perfect
location for food like this.

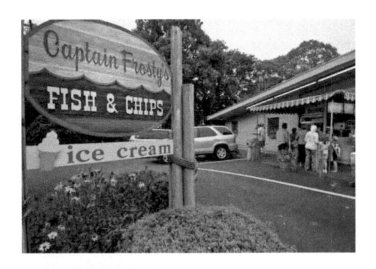

CAPTAIN FROSTY'S
219 Main St, Dennis, 508-385-8548
www.captainfrosty.com
CUISINE: Seafood/Fish & Chips
DRINKS: No Booze
SERVING: Lunch, Dinner
PRICE RANGE: $$
This casual seafood shack offers a delicious selection
of fresh seafood and burgers. Indoor and outdoor
seating. For dessert there's an ice cream shop
attached.

CAPTAIN KIDD
77 Water St, Woods Hole, 508-548-8563
www.thecaptainkidd.com
CUISINE: Seafood
DRINKS: Full Bar
SERVING: Lunch, Dinner; closed Sun, Mon & Tues
PRICE RANGE: $$

Great place for outdoor summer dining overlooking the pond. Indoor seating available. Favorites include: Kale salad with shrimp and Fish tacos.

CAPTAIN PARKER'S PUB
668 Massachusetts 28, West Yarmouth, 508-771-4266
www.captainparkers.com
CUISINE: Seafood
DRINKS: Full Bar
SERVING: Lunch, Dinner
PRICE RANGE: $$
If you're looking for hearty New England fare and great clam chowder, then this is your place. There are also great meat selections like the prime rib. And I'd be remiss if I didn't mention the bustling bar scene that for years has been luring locals and tourists alike. Follow my lead and arrive early to avoid the crowd.

CERALDI
15 Kendrick Ave, Wellfleet, 508-237-9811
www.ceraldicapecod.com
CUISINE: Italian
DRINKS: Full Bar
SERVING: Dinner, Closed Mon & Tues.
PRICE RANGE: $$$
NEIGHBORHOOD: South Wellfleet
Counter seating (comfortable chairs with real backs to them, yes!) surrounds the little kitchen on 3 sides—you can either sit here and watch as the cooks do their thing, or take a table against the walls. They only have 45 seats. This is a modern fine dining restaurant

offering a rotating 7-course menu of Italian fare that is made right in front of your eyes. Menu changes daily. Many of the ingredients have been farmed, or in the case of fish, caught just a few miles from the restaurant. Excellent wine pairings. Price is not at all unreasonable for what you get.

CHAPIN'S RESTAURANT
85 Taunton Ave, Dennis, 508-385-7000
www.chapinsrestaurant.com
CUISINE: Seafood
DRINKS: Full Bar
SERVING: Lunch, Dinner
PRICE RANGE: $$
This casual eatery offers a menu of coastal classics, pastas, steaks, and a raw bar.
Great place for the entire family. Favorites include: The Cobb Salad. End your meal with a little ice cream served at the window outside.

CHART ROOM
1 Shipyard Ln, Pocasset, 508-563-5350
www.chartroomcataumet.com
CUISINE: Seafood
DRINKS: Full Bar
SERVING: Lunch, Dinner
PRICE RANGE: $$$
This popular seafood eatery serves great dishes and the harbor view from the porch is almost as good as the food. Very busy during the summer so be prepared to wait. Regulars come back for the great New England clam chowder and the creative cocktails.

CHATHAM PIER FISH MARKET
45 Barcliff Ave, Chatham, 508-945-3474
www.chathampierfishmarket.com
CUISINE: Seafood, Sushi, Seafood Market
DRINKS: No booze
SERVING: Lunch & dinner daily
PRICE RANGE: $$
The lobster rolls here are huge. But here they also
have shrimp rolls and scallop rolls, so try one of those
instead. Also has sushi, but the menu on that is
somewhat limited (which is probably a good thing).

CHATHAM SQUIRE
487 Main St, Chatham 508-945-0945
www.thesquire.com
CUISINE: American
DRINKS: Full Bar
SERVING: Lunch, Dinner
PRICE RANGE: $$

This funky little place has a unique décor of wallpaper made from license plates. The menu is strictly classic pub fare with favorites like Lobster Bisque. Specials change daily. There's usually a wait during season but it's worth it. Occasional live music.

CHATHAM WINE BAR AND RESTAURANT
CHATHAM INN
359 Main St #2, Chatham, 508-945-1468
www.chathamwinebar.com
CUISINE: Wine Bar/American (New)
DRINKS: Wine
SERVING: Dinner
PRICE RANGE: $$$
NEIGHBORHOOD: Chatham
You can't get much better for a Cape Cod experience than to slide into this lovely charmer nestled off to the side of the Chatham Inn (which is a perfect place to stay, I might just as well say right here). It's got very fine dining in one room (choose from 3 or 4 or 5-course menus), a separate outdoor Bistro menu (Lobster & Corn Chowder) on the patio. And there's also a wine bar inside with a cozy dark atmosphere and fireplace and over 30 wines by the glass to choose from). The "fine dining" option is an upscale eatery with a steak and seafood focused menu. Favorites: Lamb shank; Chilled Watermelon Soup; Scallop Ceviche; Snake River Farms Carpaccio; Chicken & Peaches; Halibut with crispy prosciutto; Lobster tail poached in butter. But these were just samples from the menu last time I visited. Changes often. Lovely wine list. Outdoor patio, as I mentioned earlier.

CHILLINGSWORTH

2449 Main St, Brewster, 508-896-3640
www.chillingsworth.com
CUISINE: American/French
DRINKS: Full Bar
SERVING: Dinner
PRICE RANGE: $$$
Located on the 300 year-old Chillingsworth Foster estate, this high-end eatery is known as the Cape's most celebrated restaurant and one of Julia Child's favorite places on the Cape. They offer prix-fix options with a menu of classic French cuisine. Favorites include: Baked Basil Crusted Atlantic Salmon and Roasted Native Swordfish.

CIRO & SAL'S

4 Kiley Ct, Provincetown, 508-487-6444
www.ciroandsals.com
CUISINE: Italian, Seafood
DRINKS: Full Bar
SERVING: Dinner
PRICE RANGE: $$$
This go-to eatery for Northern Italian cuisine attracts fans year-round. Favorites include: Breaded veal cutlet served with spaghetti and Oven roasted salmon with a shrimp reduction sauce over risotto. Great wine cellar.

CLANCY'S RESTAURANT

8 Upper County Rd, Dennis Port, 508-394-6661
www.clancysrestaurant.com

CUISINE: Seafood
DRINKS: Full Bar
SERVING: Lunch, Dinner
PRICE RANGE: $$
For 26 years, this restaurant has served excellent seafood-influence American fare. Favorites include Fish & Chips and Chicken Parmesan. The casual eatery offers a dining room and a riverfront patio. Open year-round with creative specials changed daily.

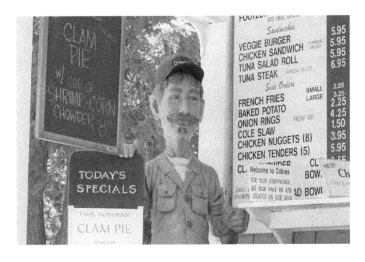

COBIE'S CLAM SHACK
3260 Main St, Brewster, 508-896-7021
www.cobies.com
CUISINE: Seafood/Fish & Chips
DRINKS: Full Bar
SERVING: Lunch, Dinner
PRICE RANGE: $$

This casual eatery has been attracting crowds since 1948 for great seafood standards, fish & chips and great burgers. Try the ice cream, it's the best on the Cape.

THE CORNER STORE
1403 Old Queen Anne Rd, Chatham, 508-432-1077
www.freshfastfun.com
CUISINE: Sandwiches/Mexican/Bakery
DRINKS: No Booze
SERVING: Breakfast/Lunch/early Dinner
PRICE RANGE: $
NEIGHBORHOOD: Chatham
Great variety of sandwiches, paninis and burritos.
Favorites: Buffalo-ranch chicken burrito and Chicken
B.L.T. Caesar Salad. Great desserts and cookies.

COTTAGE STREET BAKERY
5 Cottage St, Orleans, 508-255-2821
www.cottagestreetbakery.com
CUISINE: Bakery; sandwiches
DRINKS: No
SERVING: Daily 6 am - 5 pm
PRICE RANGE: $
Though the baked goods (cakes, pastries, pies) are the prime draw here, the other food is fine. A great selection of sandwiches and soups (like Hungarian mushroom and carrot cilantro). Salads also fresh and lively.

THE DAILY PAPER
644 West Main St, Hyannis, 508-790-8800
www.dailypapercapecod.com

CUISINE: Diner
DRINKS: No Booze
SERVING: Breakfast & Lunch
PRICE RANGE: $

This place packs them in for breakfast 7 days a week. Chef owned and operated; here you'll find they use the freshest products available. Besides the classic breakfast, favorites include Lobster Benedict and Corned Beef Hash. They also have Cape Cod Beer on draught.

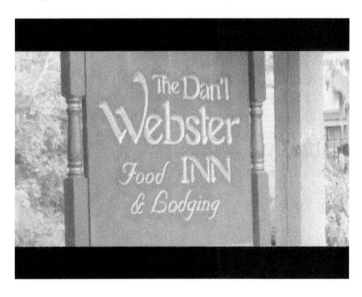

THE DAN'L WEBSTER INN & SPA
149 Main St, Sandwich, 855-958-0066
www.danlwebsterinn.com
CUISINE: American
DRINKS: Full Bar
SERVING: Breakfast, Lunch, & Dinner
PRICE RANGE: $$

This restaurant is recognized as a Distinguished Restaurant in North America and lives up to its ranking. The Inn serves in four dining rooms, each with a different décor, and the Tavern. Traditional favorites include: Prime Rib & Filet Mignon. Chef's Special Menu is constantly changing. Impressive wine list and cellar.

DEL MAR
907 Main St, Chatham, 508-945-9988
www.delmarbistro.com
CUISINE: American
DRINKS: Full Bar
SERVING: Lunch, Dinner
PRICE RANGE: $$$
This charming little spot offers a nice selection of bistro fare and seafood specials. The ambiance is welcoming and there's often live jazz. Favorites include Clams over linguini and their famous thin crust wood fired pizza.

THE DEN
697 Main St, Dennisport, 508-258-0805
https://dencapecod.com/
CUISINE: American (New)
DRINKS: Full Bar
SERVING: Lunch & Dinner
PRICE RANGE: $$
NEIGHBORHOOD: Dennis Port
Popular eatery resembling a sports bar – lots of TVs, large horseshoe bar and big open dining space. But the space is more clubby than that, with lots of dark-hued wood accents and a silver-tin type ceiling. Menu

picks: Scallops with risotto and Grilled oysters. Nice selection of wines and beers (a great many of them on tap).

DOCKSIDE RIBS N LOBSTER
110 School, Hyannis, 508-827-4355
www.thedocksidehyannis.com
CUISINE: Seafood
DRINKS: Full Bar
SERVING: Lunch, Dinner
PRICE RANGE: $$
This popular spot offers scenic waterfront dining with a menu of American classics and seafood dishes. Known for their lobster and ribs, they also serve breakfast standards and award winning fish sandwiches.

DOLPHIN RESTAURANT
3250 Main St, Barnstable, 508-362-6610
www.thedolphincapecod.com
CUISINE: Sandwiches
DRINKS: Full Bar
SERVING: Lunch, Dinner
PRICE RANGE: $$
This popular eatery features a menu of American and seafood standards. Favorites include the chicken wrap with blueberries and walnuts and Half tuna sandwich and chowder special.

DUNBAR TEA SHOP
1 Water St, Sandwich, 508-833-2485
www.dunbartea.com
CUISINE: Coffee and Tea

DRINKS: Beer and Wine Only
SERVING: Breakfast (from 8), lunch and tea till 4:30.
PRICE RANGE: $$
You'll be charmed as all get out when you enter this tea room in an old house dating back to 1740. Besides the tea, they also serve big breakfast and lunch menus with items costing sometimes less than you'd pay at a McDonald's. Great eggs Benedict, pecan smokehouse bacon, lemon poppy seed hotcakes, baked stuffed French toast. Wide variety of lovely sandwiches for lunch. Pies, cakes and pastries for tea.

EARTHLY DELIGHTS
15 W Bay Rd, Osterville, 508-420-2206
https://earthlydelightscapecod.wordpress.com/
CUISINE: Vegan
DRINKS: No Booze
SERVING: Breakfast/Lunch
PRICE RANGE: $
NEIGHBORHOOD: Osterville
Vegetarian and vegan cuisine, eco-mind sandwiches, breakfast plates, smoothies, and juices. Great freshly baked muffins every morning.

EMBARGO
453 Main St, Hyannis Port, 508-771-9700
www.embargorestaurant.com
CUISINE: Tapas/Sushi
DRINKS: Full Bar
SERVING: Lunch, Dinner
PRICE RANGE: $$
This popular eatery is a favorite with the hipster crowd. For our purposes here, that will include me! Here you'll find tapas, pizza and a lot more. The hot tapas menu runs to over 2 dozen items, from scallops wrapped in bacon to mussels a la blanca to hickory smoked baby back ribs. Big juicy steaks are also offered, including a 24-oz cowboy rib eye, along with crispy flatbreads. Favorites include Kobe Beef sliders (half price on Tuesday). Oh, and from 4:30 to 6, they have a happy hour with half-priced oysters and tapas. There's also live music in a modern lounge setting and live jazz at dinner till 9:30.

EMBER PIZZA
600 Massachusetts 28, Harwich Port, 508-430-0407
www.emberpizza.com
CUISINE: Pizza
DRINKS: Full Bar
SERVING: Dinner; closed Mon
PRICE RANGE: $$$
This popular pizzeria offers a menu of coal-fired,
thin-crust pizza, wings and pasta.
You must try the Spinach and artichoke dip and the
Gorgonzola garlic bread. Specials include the
Chicken bacon ranch pizza. This is a pizza lovers'
destination.

FANCY'S
699 Main St, Osterville, 508-428-6954
www.fancysmarket.com

CUISINE: Deli/Market
DRINKS: Beer & Wine
SERVING: 7 a.m. – 7 p.m.
PRICE RANGE: $$
NEIGHBORHOOD: Osterville
If you want to get some great take-out, come to this local market that offers a nice selection of freshly made subs, wraps and paninis, but they also have some great prepared foods, like pork tenderloin with roasted veggies, deep dish lasagna, baked salmon with a saffron cream sauce, things like that. There's also a good reasonably priced wine selection and lots of gourmet items for sale..

FANIZZI'S BY THE SEA
539 Commercial St, Provincetown 508-487-1964
www.fanizzisrestaurant.com
CUISINE: American/Seafood
DRINKS: Full Bar
SERVING: Lunch, Dinner
PRICE RANGE: $$
CUISINE: American / Seafood / Italian
DRINKS: Full Bar
SERVING: Lunch, Dinner
PRICE RANGE: $$
This locals' favorite offers and a menu of Italian classics and American seafood. Lots of towns have a restaurant like this, that started off serving classic Italian cuisine that later morphed into a combination of Italian and America. We used to call that assimilation, but that's a dirty word these days. Anyway, this is what Fanizzi might be called. So, you'll have your Chicken Piccata and your Eggplant

Parmigiana in a homemade marinara sauce, but you'll also find Braised Short Ribs and a Baked Cod with a mustard nut crust. But hey, whatever they serve here, it's damned good, I will say that. It's also right on the water, so you have spectacular views of Provincetown harbor. They even suggest you come here when the weather is at its worst. And they're right. I was in P-town one winter weekend on business and a n'or-easter hit the Cape. We came here for an early dinner, and it was thrilling to watch the waves crash up against the windows. Open 7 days a week year-round for lunch and dinner.

FAR LAND PROVISIONS
150 Bradford St, Provincetown, 508-487-0045
www.farlandprovisions.com
CUISINE: Deli/Bakery
DRINKS: No Booze
SERVING: 7 a.m. – 6 p.m.
PRICE RANGE: $
NEIGHBORHOOD: P-town
All-day deli/bakery with a nice selection of sandwiches, light fare like mac & cheese, meatloaf, and cinnamon rolls. Extensive deli section. They champion a "pier to plate" program, by which I mean they serve as much fish caught by local fishermen as they can. Their market sells beer, wine, spirits, and organic eggs.

FIN
800 Main St, Dennis, 508-385-2096
www.fincapecod.com
CUISINE: Seafood

DRINKS: Full Bar
SERVING: Dinner; closed Sun & Mon
PRICE RANGE: $$$
Located in an antique home, this high-end restaurant offers a menu of contemporary seafood. Creative wine selection offers something for everyone. Delicious desserts. Reservations recommended.

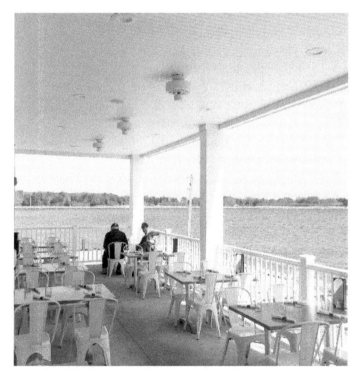

FISHERMAN'S VIEW
20 Freezer Rd, Sandwich, 508-591-0088
www.fishermensview.com
CUISINE: Seafood

DRINKS: Full bar
SERVING: Lunch & Dinner
PRICE RANGE: $$
Locals' favorite with a classic Cape Cod seafood
menu. Picks. Swordfish Steak and Striped Bass.
Lobster roll is worth getting. Lots of seating. Nice
cocktail menu.

FIVE BAYS BISTRO
825 Main St, Osterville, 508-420-5559
www.fivebaysbistro.com
CUISINE: New American
DRINKS: Full Bar
SERVING: Dinner; open Sat & Sun
PRICE RANGE: $$$
Owners Jamie Surprenant and Tim Sourza offer a
sophisticated menu of creative American cuisine.
Menu favorites include: Honey-Soy Glazed Salmon
and Braised Pork Shank. Creative wine list.

FRONT STREET
230 Commercial St, Provincetown, 508-487-9715
www.frontstreetrestaurant.com
CUISINE: Italian
DRINKS: Full Bar
SERVING: Dinner
PRICE RANGE: $$$
Kathy & Donna are the owners here in this lovely
eatery situated on the ground floor of a Victorian
mansion. Italy and southern France are the culinary
inspirations behind the food here. Amarone roasted
boneless beef short rib, truffled Sachetti alla

Carbonara, eggplant Involtini, Italian sausage with polenta, lots of great pasta creations.

GERARDI'S CAFÉ

902 Massachusetts 28, South Yarmouth, 508-394-3111
www.gerardiscafe.com
CUISINE: Italian/Gluten-free
DRINKS: Full Bar
SERVING: Dinner
PRICE RANGE: $$
This popular eatery offers a menu of classic Sicilian-style cuisine with gluten-free options. This place offers a nice dining experience for the entire family but it's romantic enough for a date night. Menu favorites include: Veal piccata and Blue crab fettuccini. The bar serves a variety of traditional Italian cocktails.

GINA'S BY THE SEA

134 Taunton Ave, Dennis, 508-385-3213
www.ginasbythesea.com
CUISINE: Italian
DRINKS: Full Bar
SERVING: Dinner; closed Mon - Wed
PRICE RANGE: $$$
This place has become a Cape Cod institution with a menu of Italian-American classics. Menu picks include: Shrimp Scampi and Eggplant Parmesan. Operating over sixty years, this place still attracts a bog loyal crowd, so reservations are recommended.

GLASS ONION

37 N Main St, Falmouth, 508-540-3730
www.theglassoniondining.com
CUISINE: American
DRINKS: Full Bar
SERVING: Dinner; closed Sun - Mon
PRICE RANGE: $$$
This elegant restaurant offers a menu of New
American cuisine. Popular choices include: Lobster
strudel appetizer and Shrimp & mussels. Global
wines and creative cocktails like their popular
watermelon mojito. No reservations.

GRUMPY'S

1408 Massachusetts 6A, East Dennis, 508-385-2911
www.grumpyscapecod.com
CUISINE: American/Diner
DRINKS: No Booze
SERVING: Breakfast, Lunch, & Dinner
PRICE RANGE: $$

Not an elegant eatery at all, just a family-owned roadside stop serving great all-American comfort food. Great breakfasts. Favorites include: Homemade corned beef hash. Try their homemade muffins (8-10 varieties). Open all year.
live Irish music (on the weekends). Menu picks include: the Belfast burger made with pulled pork and bacon.

HARVEST GALLERY WINE BAR
776 Main St, Dennis, 508-385-2444
www.harvestgallerywinebar.com
CUISINE: American
DRINKS: Beer & wine only
SERVING: Wednesday-Sundays from 4:30, when happy hour begins
PRICE RANGE: $$

The intimate, diverse gallery features more than 30 artists and their works - paintings, collages, sculptures, assemblages, textiles, photography, glass, jewelry and, of course, the culinary arts and even entertainment. Pickled local eggs; Thai crab lettuce wraps; a lovely Panini of mozzarella, roasted tomatoes, basil pesto, avocado on crusty bread; French dip (which you don't see that often anymore, and this one is good); a nice turkey melt. Good place to eat at the bar if you're alone because the staff is so friendly.

IMPUDENT OYSTER
15 Chatham Bars Ave, Chatham, 508-945-3545
www.theimpudentoyster.com
CUISINE: Seafood
DRINKS: Full Bar
SERVING: Lunch and dinner
PRICE RANGE: $$$
Set in a beautiful old house, you'll find this a romantic place for dinner. Portions are big and the

food is excellent: Sea scallops wrapped in bacon with onions, garlic and parsley; oysters Rockefeller; Vermont butternut bisque; mussels in wine; butternut ravioli; lobster croquettes; blueberry pie. The lobster roll for lunch is a treat.

INAHO
157 Rte 6A, Yarmouth Port, 508-362-5522
www.inaho-sushi.com
CUISINE: Japanese; Sushi
DRINKS: Full Bar
SERVING: Mon-Sat 4:30 pm - 10 pm
PRICE RANGE: $$$
Serves a full range of sushi as well as some hot and cold Japanese favorites like yaki gyoza (pan-fried shrimp served with vegetable dumplings) and panko scallop (kabobs of fried breaded scallops).

JT'S SEAFOOD
2689 Main St, Brewster, 508-896-3355
www.jt-seafood.com
CUISINE: Seafood
DRINKS: Beer & Wine Only
SERVING: Lunch, Dinner
PRICE RANGE: $$
This old-style New England seafood shack serves food from its counter and guests can eat inside or on the outdoor patio. Menu picks include: the Grilled Salmon and the very spectacular Cheeseburgers. For dessert they offer soft serve ice cream.

THE JERK CAFÉ

1319 Massachusetts 28, South Yarmouth, 508-394-1944

www.thejerkcafe.com

CUISINE: Caribbean

DRINKS: No Booze

SERVING: Lunch, Dinner

PRICE RANGE: $

This popular café offers a menu of Jamaican Jerk Style Caribbean cuisine. Limited seating. They're known for their great BBQ sauce and Jerk Chicken.

JIMMY'S HIDEAWAY

179 Commercial St, Provincetown, 508-487-1011

www.jimmyshideaway.com

CUISINE: American (New), Diners

DRINKS: Full Bar

SERVING: Dinner nightly from 5:30.

PRICE RANGE: $$$

NEIGHBORHOOD: Provincetown

It's hard to miss the door and trim which is painted in a bright red as you walk down a few old brick steps to a slightly subterranean and slightly romantic eatery with a dark pub-like ambience with rich wood paneling and low lighting. I love this place off season when it's snowing outside. That must be because they have very comfortable chairs at the bar, so this makes a great place to plant your butt for the evening, have a few drinks and then dinner. When the weather's all right, you can sit outside. Menu (changes with the seasons) features American fare with a European twist. Favorites: BBQ Spare Ribs; a very good Wedge salad with one of the best blue cheese dressings I've had lately; Grilled oysters with jalapeno-lemon butter; Scallops Piccata. Reservations recommended.

JOON BAR + KITCHEN
133 Commercial St, Provincetown, 508-413-9336
www.joonbar.com
CUISINE: Wine Bar/American (New)
DRINKS: Full Bar
SERVING: Lunch, Dinner, Brunch
PRICE RANGE: $$$
NEIGHBORHOOD: Provincetown
In a little white cottage, you'll find this popular modern and yet quaint eatery in a longish room with a comfortable bar (good chairs) on one side, with a few high-tops separating the bar from a long banquette against the wall. Featuring seasonal New American cuisine, with emphasis on "seasonal." Favorites: Duck Sliders on a buttermilk biscuit; Char-grilled NY Strip; Bouillabaisse made with lobster, mussels, shrimp, clams, halibut in a saffron tomato stew. Nice wine list and creative cocktails like the Joon Margarita (Tequila plata, Ancho Reyes, agave nectar, lime).

KAROO KAFE
3 Main St -Ste 32B, Eastham, 508-255-8288
www.karoorestaurants.com
CUISINE: Vegetarian/African
DRINKS: Beer & Wine Only
SERVING: Lunch, Dinner
PRICE RANGE: $$
This casual eatery offers counter service. Menu features African inspired cuisine with variety of

vegetarian and gluten-free options. Menu picks include: Ostrich burger and Chakalaka salad.

KKATIES'S BURGER BAR
334 Main St, Hyannis, 508-771-4282
www.kkaties.com
CUISINE: Burgers
DRINKS: Full bar
SERVING: Lunch & Dinner
PRICE RANGE: $$
NEIGHBORHOOD: Hyannis
Looking like a typical pub, this place is known for its burgers and they offer a variety of burgers and sandwiches. Creative cocktails.

KREAM & KONE
961 Main St, West Dennis, 508-394-0808
www.kreamnkone.com
CUISINE: Seafood
DRINKS: Beer & Wine Only
SERVING: Lunch, Dinner
PRICE RANGE: $$
Known for their fried seafood, this counter-service eatery offers casual dining by the river with a menu of seafood treats, fried clams, and sandwiches. For dessert try one of the 27 soft serve flavors.

L'ALOUETTE BISTRO
787 Massachusetts 28, Harwich Port, 508-430-0405
www.frenchbistrocapecod.com
CUISINE: French
DRINKS: Full Bar
SERVING: Dinner; closed Tues & Wed

PRICE RANGE: $$$

Located in a quaint building with dormer windows on the second floor, this casual bistro offers a menu of global cuisine, but the emphasis is on classic French cooking—that's the star at this polished, low-key place. For a starter, get the little Beignets, really just crab, corn and scallion fritters. They're delicious. Menu favorites include: the Calves liver, which you don't see very often. Here they do it right with the caramelized onions, smoked bacon, madeira sauce, mashed potatoes. My other favorite is the Duck Two Ways, by which they mean you get the grilled duck breast as well as the leg confit with a raspberry sauce. There are lots of other good dishes on this lovely menu.

LA TACODILLA
702 Ma 28, West Dennis, 508-292-8817
www.cleanslateeatery.com
CUISINE: Vegetarian/American (Traditional)
DRINKS: Beer & Wine
SERVING: Breakfast/Lunch/Dinner; closed Sun & Mon
PRICE RANGE: $$$$
NEIGHBORHOOD: West Dennis
Locals' favorite that serves healthy dishes that are served to you by the chefs. Favorites: Day Boat Scallop and Flank Steak. Nice wine pairings. Menu changes weekly.

LAMBERT'S RAINBOW FRUIT
1000 W Main St, Centerville, 508-477-0655
www.lambertsfarmmarket.com

CUISINE: Fruits & Veggies
DRINKS: Beer & Wine
SERVING: Breakfast/Lunch/Dinner
PRICE RANGE: $$$
NEIGHBORHOOD: Centerville
This place offers made-to-order giant deli
sandwiches, a salad and soup bar, deli, and a great
selection of fresh fruit, herbs, and veggies. Tasty
baked goods and desserts. Closes around 7 p.m.

LAND HO!
Route 6A at Cove Rd, Orleans, 508-255-5165
www.land-ho.com
CUISINE: American
DRINKS: Full Bar
SERVING: Lunch, Dinner
PRICE RANGE: $$
Very popular eatery during season, so try to come at
off-peak hours to avoid the crowds. Known for their
crazy décor and big baskets of chicken and fries.
Menu is mostly American comfort food but there's
also seafood. Menu picks include: Grilled chicken
club and Crab cakes.

LANDFALL
9 Luscombe Ave., Woods Hole, 508-548-1758
www.landfallwoodshole.com
CUISINE: Seafood
DRINKS: Full Bar
SERVING: Lunch and dinner, but hours vary. Call
ahead. Open April–November.
PRICE RANGE: $$
Everything used to build this place (it opened in
1946) came from "somewhere else." Every board,
plant, piece of stained glass or window has its own
story, and they'll be happy to tell it to you. Some of
the wood came from shipwrecks, some from old
houses that fell down where the wood was recycled
here. The harpoons, buoys, oars and netting were gifts
from friends. Baked stuffed lobster and the lobster

Savannah (with sherry and cream) are good. The fried scallops melt in your mouth.

THE LANES BOWL & BISTRO
9 Green St, Mashpee Commons 774-228-2291
www.lanesbowlandbistro.com
CUISINE: American
DRINKS: Full Bar
SERVING: Lunch, Dinner
PRICE RANGE: $$
This hip bowling alley offers a casual bistro with a menu of American classics, flatbread sandwiches, and hearty pizzas. Favorites include: Fried asparagus and Chicken Broccoli Alfredo pizza. Live music and an outdoor café.

LIAM MAGUIRE'S IRISH PUB AND RESTAURANT

273 Main St, Falmouth, 508-548-0285
www.liammaguire.com /
CUISINE: Irish
DRINKS: Full Bar
SERVING: Lunch, Dinner
PRICE RANGE: $$
A pub and restaurant serving classic Irish fare. Nice wine list and selection of draft beer. Known for the great burgers and huge lobster rolls. Live entertainment.

LAURA & TONY'S KITCHEN

5960 Route 6, Eastham, 508-240-6096
www.lauraandtonyskitchen.com
CUISINE: New American; Breakfast; Brunch
DRINKS: Full Bar
SERVING: Sat 7:30-noon; Sun 7:30-1 pm
PRICE RANGE: $$
Nothing simpler than this place that packs 'em in with an all-you-can-eat breakfast buffet. All the baking is done on-premise, so their excellent gooey cinnamon rolls are made fresh just before you eat them. They claim everything is so fresh they don't even have a can opener in the kitchen.

LOBSTER POT
321 Commercial St, Provincetown, 508-487-0842
www.ptownlobsterpot.com
CUISINE: Seafood
DRINKS: Full Bar
SERVING: Lunch and Dinner
PRICE RANGE: $$
Nice selection of raw bar items: oysters with sour
cream and caviar; crab claw cocktail, lobster avocado
cocktail, oysters and clams on the half shell. Main
courses hit all the right hunger spots with baked
Portuguese clams, Asian steamed littlenecks, lobster
ravioli, blackened tuna sashimi, sautéed squid. Sit in
the unpretentious room and look out over the harbor.
Spacious bar, outdoor deck.

LOCAL BREAK
4550 State Hwy, Eastham, 508-255-6100
www.local-break.com
CUISINE: American
DRINKS: Full Bar
SERVING: Dinner
PRICE RANGE: $$
Busy eatery that offers a creative menu of American cuisine. Known for their house burger and hot wings served with buffalo bleu cheese sauce. Menu of creative cocktails like the candied cranberry margarita.

THE LOCAL JUICE BAR + PANTRY
539 South St., Hyannis, 508-827-7447
www.thelocaljuice.com
CUISINE: Juices/Smoothies
DRINKS: No Booze
SERVING: Breakfast/Lunch
PRICE RANGE: $$
NEIGHBORHOOD: Hyannis
Mainly a juice and smoothie place but they also offer a variety of snacks, fresh eggs, honey, hot sauce, chocolate, and produce.

MAC'S SEAFOOD
macsseafood.com
Mac's has several old-style seafood shacks but has branched out to offer white-tablecloth service in some of his locations. Check to see which ones are close to you, as well as what kind of lunch or dining experience you're looking for. They have it all, as well as half a dozen fish markets if you want to buy

your seafood and cook it at home. Me? I prefer to let Mac's more than professional team do the shucking, do the sauteeing, do the grilling, do the broiling and do the baking. Not to mention the cleaning up. These are all good for your basic Cape Cod seafood bingeing.

MAC'S MARKET & KITCHEN
4680 RTE 6, Eastham, 508-255-6900
MAC'S FISH & LOBSTER
Cornfield Marketplace
1291 Main St, Rte 28, Chatham, 508-945-1173
MAC'S FISHHOUSE
85 Shank Painter Rd, P'town, 508-487-6227
MAC'S ON THE PIER
265 Commercial Street, Wellfleet, 508-349-9611
MAC'S SHACK
91 Commercial St, Wellfleet, 508-349-6333

MAD MINNOW
554 Main St Rt 28, Harwich Port, 774-209-3977
www.madminnow.com
CUISINE: Gastropub/American (New)
DRINKS: Full bar
SERVING: Dinner – Lunch on weekends
PRICE RANGE: $$
NEIGHBORHOOD: Harwich Port
Hangout for young hipsters serving delicious food. Favorites: Crab cakes and Tuna cannoli. Other treats include the scallop roll and gnocchi. Casual dining inside and outside on picnic tables.

MARSHLAND RESTAURANT
109 Rte 6A. Sandwich, 508-888-9824
www.marshlandrestaurant.com
CUISINE: American
DRINKS: Full Bar
SERVING: Breakfast, Lunch & Dinner; open daily
PRICE RANGE: $$
This place has been a landmark for over 50 years and open 7 days a week. The classic American menu features breakfast, lunch, and dinner. A bakery section offers muffins, pies, cakes, and cookies.

MARSHSIDE
28 Bridge St, E Dennis, 508-385-4010
www.themarshside.com
CUISINE: Seafood
DRINKS: Full Bar
SERVING: Lunch, Dinner
PRICE RANGE: $$
This casual eatery offers a creative menu of American cuisine and seafood. Sit by the windows and enjoy a great view of the marsh. Favorites include: Cobb salad and the fresh oysters. Great bar.

MATTAKEESE WHARF
273 Millway, Barnstable Harbor, 508-362-4511
www.mattakeese.com
CUISINE: Seafood
DRINKS: Full Bar
SERVING: Lunch, Dinner, & Sunday Brunch
PRICE RANGE: $$$
This place suckers people in with its great location, right on the dock. People pull up, tie off and run up to

eat and drink here. Stick to the drinks and if you're really hungry, go for the raw bar items. They're consistently good. If you want a more substantial meal, eat elsewhere.

MEWS
429 Commercial St, Provincetown, 508-487-1500
https://mewsptown.com/
CUISINE: American
DRINKS: Full Bar
SERVING: Dinner
PRICE RANGE: $$$
This popular eatery offers two levels and great views of the water. Menu favorites include: Lobster Risotto and Scallops. Nice wine list and huge vodka collection.

MISAKI
379 Main St, Hyannis, 508-771-3771
www.misakisushi.com
CUISINE: Japanese
DRINKS: Full Bar
SERVING: Dinner; closed Sun & Mon
PRICE RANGE: $$
This little Japanese eatery offers a menu of traditional sushi and creative rolls. Try their signature Cape Cod roll. Favorites in addition to sushi include: Chicken Teriyaki Grilled chicken and Vegetable Tempura. Reservations recommended.

MOM & POPS BURGERS
1603 Main St, Chatham, 774-840-4144
www.momandpopschatham.com

CUISINE: Burgers/Flipino
DRINKS: Beer & Wine
SERVING: Lunch & Dinner
PRICE RANGE: $$
NEIGHBORHOOD: Chatham
Great casual spot serving burgers, hot dogs, lumpia, frappes, craft beer and wine. Favorites: Fried chicken sandwich and the California burger. Gluten-free options.

MONTANO'S RESTAURANT
481 U.S. 6, North Truro, 508-487-2026
www.montanos.com
CUISINE: Italian
DRINKS: Full Bar
SERVING: Dinner
PRICE RANGE: $$
Cute little family-style eatery that offers a varied menu of New England fare and Italian cuisine. Favorites include: Chicken Parmigiana and Fettuccine Alfredo. Tasty homemade sangria

MOONCUSSERS TAVERN
86 Sisson Rd, Harwich Port, 508-430-1230
www.mooncusserstavern.com
CUISINE: Tapas
DRINKS: Full Bar
SERVING: Dinner
PRICE RANGE: $$$
This popular tavern is known for its tapas but also serves a variety of appetizers and entrees. Favorites include: Pan Seared Duck Breast and California Tuna

Avo Burger. Extensive wine list and great selection of martinis.

NAKED OYSTER
410 Main St, Hyannis, 508-778-6500
www.nakedoyster.com
CUISINE: New American, Seafood
DRINKS: Full Bar
SERVING: Lunch & dinner daily
PRICE RANGE: $$$
One of the best raw bars on the Cape. Lobster bisque is very good here. Oyster stew as well, with sherry, cream and shallots. Pistachio crusted Scottish salmon

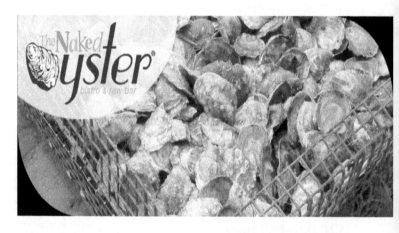

is a winner. Blackened haddock, sautéed jumbo Thai shrimp.

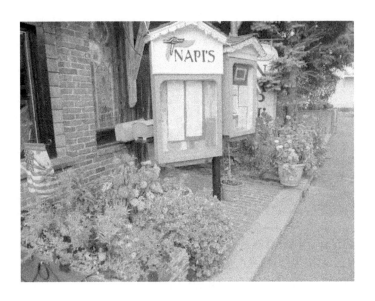

NAPI'S

7 Freeman St, Provincetown, 508-487-1145

www.napisptown.com

CUISINE: Seafood

DRINKS: Full Bar

SERVING: Dinner

PRICE RANGE: $$

This unique eatery offers an international, seafood-focused menu. Menu picks include: Chicken Picatta and Tenderloin with Brie. Vegetarian options available. Eclectic atmosphere in a venue filled with art.

OCEAN HOUSE RESTAURANT
425 Old Wharf Rd, Dennisport, 508-394-0700
www.oceanhouserestaurant.com
CUISINE: New American
DRINKS: Full Bar
SERVING: Wed-Sun 4-11(lounge opens at 4; dinner from 5)
PRICE RANGE: $$$
Very nice romantic spot. Perfect for Date Night. Sliders with "truffled ketchup" and crispy onions; orange glazed BBQ ribs; seafood bruschetta (mussels, clams, shrimp, lobster, white wine and tomato, garlic) over Tuscan bread; lump crab cake. Go a little early to get a table by the window overlooking the water.

OLD YARMOUTH INN
223 Route 6A, Yarmouth Port, 508-362-9962
www.oldyarmouthinn.com
CUISINE: American
DRINKS: Full Bar
SERVING: Lunch, Dinner
PRICE RANGE: $$$

The Inn has been an institution in Cape Cod and is known for serving the best fresh fish, shellfish, steak and pasta. Menu picks include: Chef's Vegetable Risotto and Roast Maple Leaf Farm Half Duck. Great choice for Sunday brunch. Award winning wine selection.

ORGANIC MARKET
640 Main St, Dennis Port, 508-760-3043
www.omorganicmarket.com
CUISINE: Juice Bar/Health Market
DRINKS: No Booze
SERVING: Breakfast/Lunch/Early Dinner
PRICE RANGE: $$$
NEIGHBORHOOD: Dennis Port
Health market with a juice bar. Favorites: Chicken salad sandwich and the avocado toast with red pepper flakes. Top-notch selection of products, organic vegetables, nuts, seeds and grains.

ORLEANS INN
3 Old Country Rd, Orleans, 508-255-2222
www.orleansinn.com
CUISINE: American
DRINKS: Full Bar
SERVING: Breakfast, Lunch, Dinner
PRICE RANGE: $$
A well-known hotel and restaurant filled with history dating back to 1875. A charming place for a waterfront dining offering a menu of classic Cape Cod cuisine. Menu favorites include: Blackened Salmon with a Cajun Remoulade and Chicken Picatta. Nice selection of desserts on the chef's table.

OSTERIA LA CIVETTA

133 Main St, Falmouth, 508-540-1616
www.osterialacivetta.com
CUISINE: Italian
DRINKS: Full Bar
SERVING: Lunch, Dinner
PRICE RANGE: $$
This Italian eatery offers a menu of classic housemade pastas and great Italian wine list with pretty reasonable prices. Favorites specials include: Saltimbocca alla Romana and Crema di Funghi. Try the tiramisu for dessert. It's hard to beat and made fresh daily.

OYSTER COMPANY

202 Depot St, Dennisport, 508-398-4600
www.theoystercompany.com
CUISINE: Seafood
DRINKS: Full Bar
SERVING: Lunch on Fri, Sat & Sun, Dinner nightly
PRICE RANGE: $$$
This locals' favorite also attracts the tourists who enjoy the diverse seafood menu. Favorite picks include: Oysters Rockefeller and Honey Dijon-Glazed Salmon. Also great steaks and wine list. Known for their house martinis. Reservations recommended.

PAIN D'AVIGNON

15 Hinckley Rd, Hyannis, 508-778-8588
www.paindavignon.com
CUISINE: French /Bakery

DRINKS: Full Bar
SERVING: Breakfast, Lunch, & Dinner
PRICE RANGE: $$
This European-style bakery offers a menu of French bistro fare as well as an assortment of breads and pastries. Picks include: Tartare of Beef and Grilled Spanish Octopus. You must try their sweets like the berry panna cotta and the chocolate croissant.

PALIO PIZZERIA
435 Main St, Hyannis, 508-771-7004
www.paliopizzeria.com
CUISINE: Pizza
DRINKS: Beer & Wine
SERVING: Lunch, Dinner
PRICE RANGE: $$
This casual pizzeria is known for its brick-oven pies but also serves delicious Italian fare like pastas and cannoli. Live music.

PATE'S
1260 Main St, Chatham, 508-945-9777
www.patesrestaurant.com
CUISINE: Seafood
DRINKS: Full Bar
SERVING: Lunch, Dinner
PRICE RANGE: $$$
Known for their great choice of seafood but this place is also a favorite of steak lovers. Favorites include: Baked Chatham Haddock and Filet Mignon en Brochette. Huge wine list and a separate lounge.

PB BOULANGERIE

15 Lecount Hollow Rd, Wellfleet, 508-349-1600
www.pbboulangeriebistro.com
CUISINE: French/Bakery
DRINKS: Full Bar
SERVING: Dinner on Fri & Sat, Brunch on Sun,
closed Mon - Thurs
PRICE RANGE: $$
This unique spot is half bakery and half bistro. A
great choice for either French fare or classic pastries.
Entrée picks include: Half-Cooked Smoked Salmon
and Long Island Duck Breast a l'Orange.

PEARL

250 Commercial St, Wellfleet, 508-349-2999
www.wellfleetpearl.com
CUISINE: American/Seafood
DRINKS: Full Bar
SERVING: Lunch, Dinner
PRICE RANGE: $$
This family-friendly eatery offers a classic menu of
New England standards, salads, steaks, and a raw bar.
Picks include: Teriyaki hibachi steak and Baked cod.
Busy during the summer months. Great view when
dining on the deck.

PECORINO ROMANO

605 Main St Rt 6A, Dennis, 508-694-6333
www.pecorinoromanotuscancuisine.com
CUISINE: Italian
DRINKS: Full bar
SERVING: Dinner
PRICE RANGE: $$

NEIGHBORHOOD: Dennis
Extremely popular eatery serving authentic Italian cuisine with a Tuscan flare. (I think the popularity of this place has to do with its reasonable prices as much as the so-so-quality of its food.) Menu picks: Eggplant rollantini and Veal Parmigiana. Nice selection of wines and desserts. Full menu or prix–fixe option.

PISCES
2653 Main St, Chatham, 508-432-4600
www.piscesofchatham.com
CUISINE: American
DRINKS: Full Bar
SERVING: Lunch, Dinner
PRICE RANGE: $$$
Local in a charming old house, this casual eatery offers a menu of standard American fare and Mediterranean-inspired seafood. Menu favorites include: Maine Lobster Ravioli and Yellowtail Tuna. Impressive wine list. Everything is made fresh here including the delicious desserts.

PICKLE JAR KITCHEN
170 Main St, Falmouth, 508-540-6760
www.picklejarkitchen.com
CUISINE: American
DRINKS: Full Bar
SERVING: Breakfast & Lunch; closed Tues
PRICE RANGE: $$
Popular café serving classic American comfort food. Good lunch and brunch spot with a variety of menus.

Favorites include: Pastrami seasoned smoked salmon with bagel and Blueberry muffin French toast.

POST OFFICE CAFÉ & CABARET
303 Commercial St, Provincetown, 508-487-3892
www.postofficecafe.net/
CUISINE: American (Traditional)
DRINKS: Full Bar
SERVING: Breakfast, Lunch, Dinner
PRICE RANGE: $$
NEIGHBORHOOD: Provincetown
Two-level café offering American fare on the first floor and upstairs a cabaret offering acts like RuPaul Drag Race winner Raja and The All-Male Dance Revue. Menu picks: Omelets for breakfast; Chicken quesadilla, Lobster roll and Sirloin burger for lunch; Portuguese Kale Soup, Shrimp & Grits, Homemade Meatloaf, Bone-in rib eye for dinner. A few tables under umbrellas outside in good weather. Great cocktails.

THE RED COTTAGE
36 Old Bass River Rd, South Dennis, 508-394-2923
www.redcottagerestaurant.com
CUISINE: American (Traditional) / Sandwiches
DRINKS: No Booze
SERVING: Breakfast & Lunch
PRICE RANGE: $$ **Cash only**
NEIGHBORHOOD: South Dennis
Diner-style eatery offering traditional American fare specializing in breakfast, which is why it's so popular in the morning, with superior pancakes and homemade corned beef hash. In Miami, where I'm

from, I often eat at Joe's Stone Crab early in the morning—because though they're known for stone crabs, what's not known is they serve a kick-ass breakfast (that's also very cheap). I go because the quality is so good. The same for this place—their bacon is cut thick—9 slices to the pound, and comes in Applewood, Black Pepper or Cajun flavors. The eggs and everything else is of the highest quality. Oh, and though their regular home fries are plenty good enough, specify that you want their "Red Cottage Home Fries," a little cut above—these mix the usual grilled potatoes with lots more: onions, tomatoes, ham, green peppers & mushrooms combined with special spices and topped with lemon Hollandaise sauce. (In fact, this side dish is a meal in itself.) Cash only.

THE RED INN
15 Commercial St, Provincetown, 508-487-7334
www.theredinn.com
CUISINE: New American
DRINKS: Full bar; happy hour from 2:30 to 5; raw bar specials
SERVING: Lunch and dinner
PRICE RANGE: $$
This inn (from 1915) has a great restaurant: pan roasted local cod on a bed of rosemary potatoes and applewood bacon. The lamb chops are tops as well. The bar here makes a great place to grab a drink and absorb the atmosphere, or even better, enjoy the sunset.

RED NUN BAR & GRILL

746 Main St, Chatham, 508-348-0469
673 Main St, Dennis Port, 508-394-BUOY (2869)
www.rednun.com
CUISINE: American
DRINKS: Full bar
SERVING: Lunch and dinner daily from 11:30,
except Sunday, when it's closed
PRICE RANGE: $$
Situated in a lovely red clapboard house with indoor
and outdoor seating is this fun place. Serves up fried
lobster; stuffed Quahogs; beer battered onion rings;
fish tacos; fried or baked scallops; 6 or 7 burger
creations (including the option to "build your own");
pulled pork sandwiches. (Their location in Dennis
Port is in a simple brick building, but the food and
vibe make up for the lackluster setting.)

RED PHEASANT INN

905 Main St (Rte 6A), Dennis, 508-385-2133
www.redpheasantinn.com
CUISINE: New American
DRINKS: Full bar
SERVING: Tues-Sun, dinner only from 5
PRICE RANGE: $$
A converted 200-year-old barn is the setting for this
rustic charmer serving up exciting creative dishes: the
chowder here has cherrystones and scallops with
thyme; white bean crostini; there's a nightly game
special, like venison or elk; roasted rack of lamb with
gratin potatoes & panna cotta.

RED'S AT SEA CREST BEACH HOTEL

350 Quaker Rd, North Falmouth, 508-356-2136
www.seacrestbeachhotel.com
CUISINE: American
DRINKS: Full Bar
SERVING: Lunch, Dinner
PRICE RANGE: $$
Located in Sea Crest Beach Hotel, this favorite seafood spot also serves classic American fare. Great ocean view with poolside & porch dining. Great Lobster, BBQ and pizza.

RELISH

93 Commercial St, Provincetown, 508-487-8077
www.ptownrelish.com/
CUISINE: Bakery; deli
DRINKS: No booze
SERVING: Breakfast and lunch (till 3 weekdays, till 5 weekends).
PRICE RANGE: $$
Dozens of baked goods: double fudge brownies, chocolate dipped macaroons, triple chip cookies, cupcakes, pies, you name it. They also have an excellent selection of delicious sandwiches for lunch. Director John Waters loves this place.

ROSS' GRILL

237 Commercial St, Provincetown, 508-487-8878
www.rossgrillptown.com
CUISINE: American
DRINKS: Full Bar
SERVING: Lunch, Dinner; closed Mon - Wed
PRICE RANGE: $$$

Located on the harbor front, this casual grill offers a menu of New American cuisine.

Menu favorites include: Cape Cod Seafood Stew and Fresh Vegan Ravioli with Marinara Sauce.

Impressive wine list with over 75 wines served by the glass. Tapas & Raw Bar Happy Hour. Reservations recommended.

RUGGIE'S BREAKFAST & LUNCH

707 Main St, Harwich, 508-432-0625
www.ruggiescapecod.com
CUISINE: Breakfast/Sandwiches
DRINKS: No Booze
SERVING: Breakfast & Lunch
PRICE RANGE: $$
Located in historic Harwich, this little café is a nice choice for breakfast or a quick lunch. Menu favorites

include: Chicken & Waffles and Breakfast Nachos
with eggs.
Open year round.

SAGAMORE INN
1131 MA-6A, Sagamore, 508-888-9707
www.sagamoreinncapecod.com
CUISINE: American (New)
DRINKS: Full Bar
SERVING: Lunch & Dinner; Breakfast on weekends
PRICE RANGE: $$
New owners, Michael and Suzanne Bilodeau,
celebrate the old owners by serving all the old
favorites. Classic roadhouse atmosphere with a great
menu of comfort food – mostly Italian and seafood.
Creative desserts.

SAM DIEGO'S
950 Iyannough Rd, Hyannis, 508-771-8816
www.samdiegos.com
CUISINE: Mexican
DRINKS: Full Bar
SERVING: Lunch, Dinner
PRICE RANGE: $$
This Americanized Mexican eatery offers a full menu
of award-winning Mexican and Tex-Mex selections.
Patio dining in warm months.

SESUIT HARBOR CAFÉ
357 Sesuit Neck Rd, Dennis, 508-385-6134
https://sesuit-harbor-cafe.com/
CUISINE: Seafood
DRINKS: No booze, but you can BYOB

SERVING: Breakfast (from 7am), lunch and early dinner daily till dusk.

PRICE RANGE: $$ / **cash only**

A real seafood shack that's a locals' hangout. (They come for the lobster roll—there's none better. Comes with fries and slaw. It is worth a drive.) The plate of scallops is very good. A half-order is more than sufficient. The place is tucked away in a marina here on the north shore. You order inside, take a number, go out and sit at a picnic table till they bring your food to you. If you opt for breakfast, go for the lobster omelette. Quite a full menu. Nothing fancy. Lots of boat traffic. Repeat: cash only.

SIENA

17 Steeple St, Mashpee, 508-477-5929
www.siena.us
CUISINE: Italian/Pizza
DRINKS: Full Bar
SERVING: Lunch, Dinner
PRICE RANGE: $$

A locals' favorite that welcomes tourists during season. Menu features Roman-style pizzas and hearty Italian fare. Great handpicked wine list. Good selection of gluten-free options.

SIMPLY DIVINE PIZZA

271 Main St, Falmouth, 508-548-1222
www.divinepizza.com
CUISINE: Pizza
DRINKS: Full Bar
SERVING: Lunch, Dinner
PRICE RANGE: $$

This casual pizza joint offers hand-tossed thin-crust pizza, pastas, and sandwiches. The Neopolitan pizza is a favorite. Nice wine list and selection of regional craft beers.

SIR CRICKET'S FISH & CHIPS
38 Rte 6A, Orleans, 508-255-4453
https://nausetfishandlobsterpool.com/sir-crickets-fish-n-chips
CUISINE: Seafood
DRINKS: No booze
SERVING: Lunch and dinner daily.
PRICE RANGE: $$
Seafood shack with all the usual suspects: platters and rolls of fried clams, scallops, oysters, shrimp.

SPANKY'S CLAM SHACK
138 Ocean St #115, Hyannis Port, 508-771-2770
www.spankysclamshack.com
CUISINE: Seafood
DRINKS: Full Bar
SERVING: Lunch, Dinner
PRICE RANGE: $$
This casual family-friendly eatery offers a menu of New England seafood standards. Favorites include: Lobster salad and Roasted Atlantic Swordfish. Extensive cocktail menu. Kids menu and gift shop.

SPINNAKER
2019 Main St, Brewster, 508-896-7644
www.spincape.com
CUISINE: Italian
DRINKS: Full Bar

SERVING: Dinner, Lunch (Tues – Sat)
PRICE RANGE: $$
NEIGHBORHOOD: Brewster
Casual beachy-chic eatery serving gourmet Italian
fare. There are 3 different rooms you can dine in,
casual and cozy. Menu picks: Lobster fritters are
crispy and delicious with a hot dipping sauce,
Chatham mussels are succulent and the dates stuffed
with gorgonzola and wrapped in bacon are just about
the best I've ever had. Save room for the brioche
bread pudding served with vanilla ice cream.

SPOON AND SEED
12 Thornton Dr, Hyannis, 774-470-4634
www.spoonandseed.com
CUISINE: American (Traditional)/Comfort food
DRINKS: No Booze
SERVING: Breakfast/Lunch
PRICE RANGE: $$
NEIGHBORHOOD: Hyannis
Rustic cafe offering a menu of locally sourced
American comfort food. Great breakfast options like
the Porto-Benny – their jazzed up version of Eggs
Benedict. Favorites: Eggs N' Hash. Not your typical
diner fare.

SUNBIRD KITCHEN
85 Rt 6A, Orleans, 508-237-0354
www.sunbirdprovisions.com
CUISINE: American (New)/Seafood
DRINKS: Full bar
SERVING: Breakfast/Lunch/Dinner; closed Tues
PRICE RANGE: $$

NEIGHBORHOOD: Orleans
Café offering up locally sourced American cuisine with a twist. Favorites: Smoked mozzarella cheese & kimchi and Bass & beans. Hipster crowd.

SWEET TOMATOES PIZZA
461 Station Ave, South Yarmouth, 508-394-6054
www.sweettomatoescapecod.com
CUISINE: Pizza
DRINKS: Beer & Wine Only
SERVING: Lunch, Dinner
PRICE RANGE: $$
A popular pizza chain that attracts locals and tourists. Several locations in the area.

TERRA LUNA
104 Shore Rd, North Truro, 508-487-1019
https://terralunarestaurant.com
CUISINE: Italian; New American
DRINKS: Full Bar
SERVING: Breakfast, Tue-Sun 7-12; dinner 5-10
PRICE RANGE: $$
Fra Diablo with mussels and shrimp. Romantic setting. Note that it's also open for breakfast. Romantic setting.

TIKI PORT
Capetown Plaza, 714 Iyanough Rd, Hyannis Port, 508-771-5220
www.tikiport.com
CUISINE: Chinese
DRINKS: Full Bar
SERVING: Lunch, Dinner

PRICE RANGE: $$
This long-time favorite offers a giant menu of
Chinese and Polynesian cuisine. Bar offers tropical
drinks from the South Pacific. Luncheon specials.
Known as Cape Cod's #1 Chinese restaurant.

TIN PAN ALLEY
269 Commercial St, Provincetown, 508-487-1648
www.tinpanalleyptown.com
CUISINE: Seafood, American (New)
DRINKS: Full Bar
SERVING: Lunch & Dinner
PRICE RANGE: $$
Posh eatery in the center of P-town with a creative
menu. Overlooks the ocean. Also has patio dining and
a lounge (piano bar) with live entertainment from 9
p.m. Has a popular happy hour. Menu favorites
include: Scallops with pea risotto and Swordfish with
risotto.

TREVI CAFÉ & WINE BAR
25 Market St, Mashpee, 508-477-0055
www.trevicafe.com
CUISINE: Contemporary Mediterranean Cuisine
DRINKS: Full Bar
SERVING: Lunch, Dinner
PRICE RANGE: $$
This is a wine bar with a menu of Contemporary
Mediterranean cuisine. The bar offers a list of wines
over 250 wines from around the world. Tapas and
Vegetarian options.

TUGBOATS
11 Arlington St, West Yarmouth, 508-775-6433
www.tugboatscapecod.com
CUISINE: Seafood/American
DRINKS: Full Bar
SERVING: Lunch, Dinner
PRICE RANGE: $$
This family-friendly seafood eatery offers waterfront
and deck seating with great marina views. Menu
favorites include: Baked Seafood Macaroni & Cheese
and Baked Native Sea Scallops. Great desserts like
Cape Cod Mud Pie.

TWENTY-EIGHT ATLANTIC
Wequassett Resort, 2173 Rte 28, Harwich, 508-430-
3000
www.wequassett.com/dining - /twenty-eight/
CUISINE: Seafood
DRINKS: Full Bar
SERVING: Breakfast 7-11; dinner 6-11
PRICE RANGE: $$$
Dressy, so no shorts or flip-flops. One of the more
elegant spots on the Cape located in the Wequassett
Resort. Large windows overlook Pleasant Bay. Hand-
blown chandeliers, nautical etchings. Paella risotto;
lobster & mushroom ravioli; halibut, roasted local
cod; lobster braised in butter; beef tenderloin poached
in port wine.

VAN RENSSELAER'S RESTAURANT & RAW BAR
1019 U.S. 6, Wellfleet, 508-349-2127
www.vanrensselaers.com

CUISINE: Seafood
DRINKS: Full Bar
SERVING: Breakfast, Lunch, & Dinner
PRICE RANGE: $$
Popular seafood eatery that also serves breakfast in the summer. Nice varied menu of Cape Cod fare specializing in fresh seafood. Breakfast in the summer. Dinner with Early Bird specials. Raw Bar.

VINING'S BISTRO ON MAIN
593 Main St, Chatham, 508-945-5033
www.bistroonmainchatham.com
CUISINE: American
DRINKS: Full Bar
SERVING: Lunch - weekends, Dinner nightly; closed Mon & Tues
PRICE RANGE: $$$
Restaurateur Steve Vining's latest incarnation, this bistro offers a menu of internationally inspired food. Favorites include: Caramelized Onion Crusted Black Pearl Organic Salmon and Hickory Braised Cider Brined Pork Shank. Great specials.

WICKED OYSTER
50 Main St, Wellfleet, 508-349-3455
www.thewickedo.com
CUISINE: Seafood; steaks, chops
DRINKS: Full Bar
SERVING: Breakfast 7:30 to noon; no lunch in
season; dinner from 5.
PRICE RANGE: $
Buttermilk waffles for breakfast; nice range of
omelets; huevos rancheros. For dinner, check out the
oyster tart as a starter. The grilled marinated pork
chop here is served over cheesy grits, topped with
stewed apples & pears.

WICKED RESTAURANT & WINE BAR
35 South St, Mashpee, 508-477-7422
www.wickedrestaurant.com
CUISINE: Pizza/American/Gluten-Free
DRINKS: Full Bar
SERVING: Lunch, Dinner

PRICE RANGE: $$
This stylish eatery offers a creative menu of pizza and American fare. Gluten-free options. Favorites include: Sweet Ginger Soy Grilled Salmon and Fresh Cavatelli Pasta. Impressive wine list.

WILD GOOSE TAVERN
512 Main St, Chatham, 508-945-5590
www.wildgoosetavern.com
CUISINE: American
DRINKS: Full Bar
SERVING: Lunch, Dinner
PRICE RANGE: $$
This casual eatery offers a menu of fresh seafood and American cuisine. Impressive selection of sandwiches, burgers and salads. Favorites include: Chicken & Spinach Burger and Faroe Islands Salmon. Creative cocktail list.

WINSLOW'S TAVERN
316 Main St, Wellfleet, 508-349-6450
www.winslowstavern.com
CUISINE: American
DRINKS: Full Bar
SERVING: Lunch - weekends, Dinner – nightly; closed Mon
PRICE RANGE: $$
Located in an 1880's mansion, this popular tavern offers a varied menu of New American cuisine and seafood favorites. Favorites include: Tail And Claw Lobster Roll and Grilled Chicken Paillard. Reservations recommended.

YARDARM

48 S Orleans Rd, Orleans, 508-255-4840

www.the-yardarm.com

CUISINE: Seafood/American/Pub

DRINKS: Full Bar

SERVING: Lunch, Dinner

PRICE RANGE: $$

A popular hangout for locals and tourists, this eatery offers a menu of American classics and seafood along with bar snacks. Favorites include: Clam strips and BBQ ribs. TVs to watch sports.

YARMOUTH HOUSE

335 Massachusetts 28, West Yarmouth, 508-771-5154

www.yarmouthhouse.com

CUISINE: Seafood/Steakhouse

DRINKS: Full Bar

SERVING: Breakfast, Lunch, & Dinner

PRICE RANGE: $$$

Popular dining spot with great views of the water mill. Nice varied menu featuring items like lobster and prime rib. If you're a fan of seafood and steak try the Filet Mignon a la Neptune (lobster on top with hollandaise sauce). Family friendly.

ZOE'S PIZZA
38 Bates Rd, Mashpee, 508-477-1711
www.zoespizza.com
CUISINE: Pizza
DRINKS: No Booze
SERVING: Lunch, Dinner
PRICE RANGE: $
Popular pizzeria with a menu of pizzas, calzones,
pastas and homemade lasagna. Favorites include their
BBQ chicken pizza and the classic Hawaiian pizza.

Chapter 5
WHAT TO SEE & DO

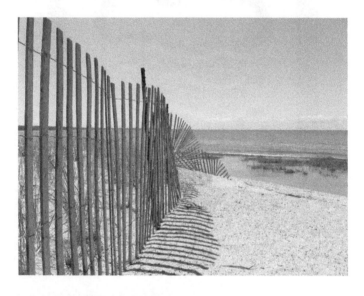

ART'S DUNE TOURS
4 Standish Street, Provincetown, 508-487-1950
www.artsdunetours.com
There are miles of sand dunes near Provincetown and
a real treat is going out there on one of Art's Dune
Tours. They'll show you the "artists' shacks" where

people like Tennessee Williams and Eugene O'Neill went to work on their writing. (These shacks are still rented to artists.) In addition to daily tours of the dunes, Art's offers Race Point lighthouse tours and sunset tours that include a clambake served picnic style.

BEACHCOMBER BOAT TOURS
174 Crowell Rd, Chatham, 508-945-5265
www.sealwatch.com
You can't miss the bright-yellow boats operated by Beachcomber Boat Tours. They'll take you out to see the seals on the beaches, fishing on the flats or they can do sunset cruises. They have trips to the Outer Beaches where you can go for a fantastic picnic. They can customize most tours. Departs from Chatham's Municipal Fishing Pier on Shore Road.

BEACHES
There are hundreds of beaches on Cape Cod, and everybody has a favorite one.
Among the ones we like:

Cape Cod National Seashore that runs for 40 miles from Chatham north to Provincetown. President Kennedy ordered it protected in 1961. It's idyllic. Another great spot is **North Beach,** which is on a sandbar off Chatham, but you need a boat to get to it. **Race Point** in Provincetown. You can often see whales from this beach.

Old Silver Beach in North Falmouth rolls out in a long crescent. Calm and quiet, but lots of families show up here.

Craigville Beach in Hyannis is also called **Muscle Beach** for obvious reasons. If you got it, here's where you flaunt it.

Nauset Beach in East Orleans is a grand beach. While here, be sure to get some fried seafood at **Liam's**, and don't forget their famous onion rings. **Sandy Neck Beach** in West Barnstable and Sandwich runs 6 miles, featuring beautiful dunes and lots of birds.

Longnook Beach, Truro, **508-487-6983.**
http://www.truro-ma.gov/beach-office/pages/longnook-beach
This is a beach favored by longtime P-town resident filmmaker John Waters.
"The most beautiful beach, with this giant cliff," he says. "It looks like the credits to soap operas. It has real waves. Parking is nearly impossible, so I hitchhike there. I also just like hitchhiking. I have an old, handwritten sign that says 'Longnook' on one side and 'Provincetown' on the other. I get a ride in a second."

SUNSET (WHERE TO BE)
There are dozens of great places to watch the sun go down, somewhat of a "fun" thing to do out on the Cape.

Race Point Beach
Provincetown
Like a bunch of hippies in Key West, sunset-seekers
applaud when the sun dips below the horizon here.
(Yes, because of the unusual shape of the Outer Cape,
the sun sets into the water, an oddity on the East
Coast.)

Red Inn
Provincetown
An excellent place to watch the sun go down. Go
before the crowds arrive so you can get a table and
enjoy an early dinner.

Chart Room Restaurant
Cataumet
Grab a glass of wine or a beer and watch the sun go
down with what's usually a large crowd.

Rock Harbor
Orleans
They have trees growing out of the water that add a
striking feature to the sunset.

CAPE COD BUMPER BOATS
322 Rte 28, Harwichport, 508-430-1155
www.capecodbumperboats.com
There's a spray canon in the bumper boat pool that
when you hit it with your boat sets off a big water
spray.

CAPE COD LAVENDER FARM
41 Weston Woods Rd, Harwich, 508-432-8397
www.capecodlavenderfarm.com
They have 14,000 plants on this, one of the largest
lavender farms on the East Coast. Cynthia and
Matthew Sutphin live on the property. They have
lavender shampoo, sage body butter, fragrance sticks,
Dead Sea salts, soap, lavender soy candles, and
sachets, even lavender-lemon marmalade.

CAPE COD MUSEUM OF NATURAL HISTORY
869 Main St, Brewster, 508-896-3867
www.ccmnh.org
Has guided tours every Wednesday along the dunes
and into the salt marshes; lots of different programs,
like Birdwatching for Beginners, Tuesday Tweets,
another birdwatching program. They have several

trails, the most popular of which is John Wing Trail that runs 1.3 miles through coastal pitch woodlands, across a salt marsh to Wing's Island before descending through a salt marsh swale to the barrier beach and tidal pools of Cape Cod Bay.

CAPE COD RAIL TRAIL
Rt 134, South Dennis, **508-896-3491**
www.capecodbikeguide.com/railtrail.asp
This trail follows an old railroad right-of-way for 22 miles, beginning in Dennis and going through the towns of Harwich, Brewster, Orleans, Eastham and Wellfleet. Has a paved surface. Lots of places to stop along the way for a bite or a drink.

CAPE PLAYHOUSE
820 Main St, Dennis, 508-385-3838
www.capeplayhouse.com
This famous playhouse has been offering theatre on Cape Cod for about 90 years. Claims to be American's oldest professional theatre. Many stars worked here, including Bette Davis, Humphrey Bogart, Gregory Peck, Helen Hayes, Tallulah Bankhead, among many others in its long history. (Bette Davis was an usher here before she was an actress.)

THE EDWARD GOREY HOUSE
8 Strawberry Ln, Yarmouth Port, 508-362-3909
www.edwardgoreyhouse.org
This is the former home of the famous illustrator. (If you've ever read a copy of "The New Yorker," you've seen his work.) He died of a heart attack in an

upstairs room and it was decided to turn the house into a museum honoring his work. Proceeds go to animal welfare, one of Gorey's passions. The artist had 6 cats. After the last of the 6 died, their ashes were mixed with his and scattered around the grounds.

FISHING
Bay Lady II
587 Commercial St, Provincetown, 508-487-9308
For larger parties or individual fishermen.
Ginny G
MacMillan Pier, Provincetown, 508-246-3656
Deep sea fishing.

FLYER'S BOAT SHOP & RENTAL
131 Commercial St, Provincetown, 508-487-0898
www.flyersboats.com
Here they have a boat called the **Long Point Shuttle** that takes you out to the very end of Cape Cod, Long Point. The Cape really does hook all the way around, completely enclosing P-town Harbor, thus making it the sheltered anchorage it is. At the very tip is Long Point Lighthouse. There are no roads, off-road tracks or trails to get there. It's a 3-mile hike if you want to do it on foot. Or, you can take a ride on one of their boats to go see this isolated spot. It only takes a few minutes to get there by boat, and it's a lot of fun.

GOOSE HUMMOCK
15 Rt 6A, Orleans, 508-255-0455
www.goosehummockshops.com

This really is a one-stop-shop for the outdoorsman. Whether you're looking for a guided kayak tour or a sport fishing charter, this is the place. The offer sales, service and rentals on all sorts of marine equipment, boats, fishing equipment, a wide range of guns for the hunter. Clothing, accessories, you name it.

HERITAGE MUSEUM & GARDENS
67 Grove St, Sandwich, 508-888-3300
www.heritagemuseumsandgardens.org
HOURS: 10 am – 5 pm, daily
ADMISSION fee applies.
Here you'll find beautifully landscaped rhododendron gardens and three galleries. On-site café. On the grounds is the Old East Mill, a restored windmill built in 1800. The galleries feature rotating exhibitions as well as the permanent carousel featuring a working 1908 carousel.

JOHN F. KENNEDY HYANNIS MUSEUM
397 Main St, Hyannis, 508-790-3077
www.jfkhyannismuseum.org
This interesting little museum is dedicated to showing you how Kennedy spent his time on Cape Cod. The vintage photos used in the rotating exhibits provide a clear view of the lifestyle the President enjoyed when he visited Cape Cod.

KETTLE PONDS
So-called kettle ponds, or "kettle holes" were formed when glaciers retreated toward Canada during the last Ice Age. (Thoreau's Walden Pond is a kettle pond.)

They make great places for fresh-water swims.
There's **LONG POND** in South Yarmouth, located
on Indian Memorial Drive off Station Ave.

Others are **GULL POND**, **FLAX POND** and **CLIFF
POND**. Check out Jack's Boat rental where you can
rent pedal boats, sea cycles, canoes, kayaks and the
like on these ponds. http://jacksboatrental.com/ - Call
Jack on 508-349-9808 for more. Rt. 6 at Cahoon
Hollow Road and at Gull Pond, Wellfleet.

MARTHA'S VINEYARD / NANTUCKET FERRY
STEAMSHIP AUTHORITY
http://www.vineyardferries.com
508-228-0262
Frequent daily departures aboard the Steamship
Authority from Wood's Hole to Martha's Vineyard
and from Hyannis to Nantucket. $50 round-trip; half
for kids.

MASS AUDUBON WELLFLEET BAY WILDLIFE SANCTUARY
291 State Hwy Rt 6, South Wellfleet, 508-349-2615
www.massaudubon.org
In their 1,200 acres of salt marshes and pine forest,
the good folks here offer bird and seal watching tours,
as well as canoe trips.

MONOMOY NATIONAL WILDLIFE REFUGE
30 Wikis Way, Chatham, 508-945-0594
www.fws.gov/refuge/Monomoy/

This is a fascinating protected area for birds and other wildlife. The goal when they established this preserve was to provide habitat for migratory birds. The size of the refuge is 7,604 acres, with varied habitats of oceans, salt and freshwater marshes, dunes, freshwater ponds, and some historic manmade structures, such as the Monomoy Point Light and keeper's quarters (decommissioned but open to the public).

OCEAN QUEST

100 Water St, Woods Hole, 508-385-7662
www.oceanquest.org
WEBSITE DOWN AT PRESSTIME
They have a series of oceangoing cruises that you might enjoy. One is called Hands On Discovery Cruises. Why is the sea green? You get to take a sample of seawater from the ocean and find out why. When you swallow a little seawater while swimming, you'll learn just what you took in. Lots of interesting things like those.

PILGRIM MONUMENT

1 High Pole Hill Road
Provincetown, 508-487-1310
www.pilgrim-monument.org
If the pilgrims could see what's become of P-town, Cole Porter's lyric "Plymouth Rock would land on them" would come true. This museum commemorates the Mayflower Pilgrims' "first landing" in P-town and the writing of the Mayflower Compact.

THE SANDWICH GLASS MUSEUM

129 Main St, Sandwich, 508-888-0251
www.sandwichglassmuseum.org

You'll come here to see the wonderful collection of vintage glass, but you'll find out that the "glass industry" was quite important to the town of Sandwich. HOURS: Summer hours, 9:30 a.m. - 5 p.m. Winter hours, 9:30 a.m. – 4 p.m.
ADMISSION: Moderate admission; tours available. This glass museum features a wide range of rare glass, including glass from the local Boston & Sandwich Glass Factory. On-site live glass blower, and exhibitions detailing the creation of rare glass. The museum exhibits nearly 5,000 pieces of glass. Museum shop on site.

SCHOOLHOUSE GALLERY

494 Commercial St, Provincetown, 508-487-4800

www.galleryschoolhouse.com
Thursday-Monday 11-5 & by appointment
The emphasis here is on promoting and exhibiting the
work of some 50 Outer Cape and national artists in
the fields of painting, photography and printmaking.
The gallery takes its name from the old schoolhouse
(built in 1844) in which it's located.

SHINING SEA BIKEWAY
Pin Oak Way, Falmouth
www.capecodbikeguide.com
This bike path follows the original route of the New
York, New Haven and Hartford Railroad that ran
from Buzzards Bay through Falmouth, around Woods
Hole and into Falmouth Station. In the early '70s, the
town bought the right-of-way, tore up the tracks and
created this bike path. With an addition in 2009, the
path now runs 7.4 miles. Perfect for families.
Bikeway gets its name from a lyric in the song
"America the Beautiful," which as it happens was
written by Katharine Lee Bates, a Falmouth native.
Who knew?

SPOHR GARDENS
45 Fells Rd, Falmouth, 508-548-0623
www.spohrgardens.org
Open year-round.
Situated around Oyster Pond is this 6-acre garden
featuring thousands of daffodils, azaleas,
rhododendrons and daylilies. Founded by Margaret
and Charles D. Spohr in the 1950s when they began
creating the gardens around the home they lived in.
When they died, a trust kept the place open for

visitors to enjoy. You could leave worse things behind.

SUSAN BAKER MEMORIAL MUSEUM
46 Shore Rd, North Truro, 508-487-2557
No Website
Gallery showcasing the artist's works.

THEATRE
Cape Cod has a large number of theatres -- one in nearly every town as well as a number of festivals including the **Provincetown Fringe Festival** and **Eventide Arts Festival.** Check the local listings to see what's playing during your visit. You'll be amply rewarded.

TRURO CENTER FOR THE ARTS AT CASTLE HILL
10 Meetinghouse Rd, Truro, 508-349-7511
www.castlehill.org
A workshop for the arts offering classes in painting, photography, printmaking, sculpture, ceramics, photography, jewelry and writing. Summer program features readings and lectures by leading figures in the arts.

TRURO VINEYARDS OF CAPE COD
11 Shore Rd, North Truro, 508-487-6200
www.trurovineyardsofcapecod.com
This may be the last place you expect to find a winery, but in this farmhouse from the 1830s you can taste wines more interesting than good. The better wines are the Triumph and Zinfandel. In their

"Lighthouse Series," some wines (Cape Blush, Cranberry Red and Diamond White) are sold in bottles shaped like a lighthouse. In the gift shop, take special note of their wine jellies, which are really good.

WELLFLEET DRIVE-IN THEATRE
51 Rt 6, Wellfleet, 508-349-7176
www.wellfleetcinemas.com/drive-in-theatre
A blast from the past. But don't expect B or C movies. They offer first-run double features are all summer. If your kids have never been to a drive-in, show them what it was like.

WELLFLEET HARBOR ACTORS THEATER
2357 Old Route 6 Rd,, Wellfleet, 508-349-9428
www.what.org
They have a new $7 million stage named after longtime honorary board chairwoman Julie Harris. Top-notch professional theatre. See what's playing when you're on the Cape.

WHALE WATCHING

Whereas this area used to be the launching point for whalers to go to sea to kill the whales, now there are companies that will take you out to watch them.

Alpha Whale Watch
Provincetown, 508-221-5920
They can take up to 6 passengers at a time.

Cape Cod Whale Watch
239 Commercial St, Provincetown, 508-487-4079

SeaSalt Charters
MacMillan Pier, Provincetown, 508-444-2732
Though they really specialize in fishing trips (striped bass and bluefish), they'll do whale watching private charters.

WHITE CEDAR SWAMP TRAIL
Marconi Beach
Wellfleet
Six miles north of Salt Pond Visitor Center, off Route 6 in Wellfleet.
www.nps.gov/caco/planyourvisit/marconi-beach.htm
An observation platform at the Marconi Station site offers an excellent overview of the Outer Cape, including both ocean and bay.
The Atlantic White Cedar Swamp Trail is a 1-1/2 mile nature trail that descends gradually in elevation into the swampy environment that hosts Atlantic white cedar and red maple trees. The trail offers an excellent view of different plant communities, starting with heathlands, then stunted pitch pines and bear oak, taller pitch pines and black and white oaks, and finally the white cedar-red maple community.
Interesting Facts:
The Marconi Area obtained its name from the famous Italian inventor, Marconi. From a site here, Marconi successfully completed the first transatlantic wireless communication between the U.S. and England in 1903.
Here, the outer beach is famous for its then steep, forty-foot sand cliff (or scarp) located behind it. Swimmers and beach walkers feel a sense of solitude here because the scarp and ocean provide an unbroken, pristine natural scene in all directions.

WOODS HOLE SCIENCE AQUARIUM
166 Water St, Woods Hole, 508-495-2001
www.nefsc.noaa.gov/aquarium/

They have some 140 marine animals populating the Northeast and Middle Atlantic waters. Seal feedings at 11 and 4 most days.

Chapter 6
SHOPPING & SERVICES

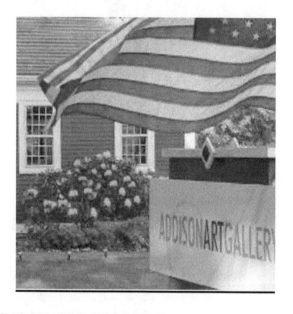

ADDISON ART GALLERY
43 South Orleans Rd, Orleans, Cape Cod, 508-255-6200
www.addisonart.com
Charming gallery set in an old red house exhibiting a beautiful collection of artists.

BED OF ROSES

281 Commercial St #3, Provincetown, 508-487-5700
www.bed-of-roses-provincetown.com
Floral designs for every occasion. Fresh and silk
flower arrangements. Live plants, silk, succulents, a
wide variety of vases and pots.

BIRD WATCHER'S GENERAL STORE

36 Rt 6A, Orleans, 508-255-6974
36 Cranberry Hwy
www.birdwatchersgeneralstore.com
You'll think you walked into an aviary when you
enter this place—all the sounds of birds! Everything
for the bird lover: window feeders, thistle feeders,
birdbaths, field guides, binoculars, bird games and
puzzles, sock with bird designs, bird earrings. It never
ends.

THE BREWSTER STORE

1935 Main St, Brewster, 508-896-3744
www.brewsterstore.com
What had been a church in 1852 became a general
store in 1866 and it's been that ever since. In 1990
they emptied out the entire place did a top to bottom
refurbishment. This is a real general store, so you can
buy groceries, gifts, things for the home you might
otherwise go to a hardware store to get, clothing, you
name it. In the back of the first floor, they've opened
the **Brewster Scoop**, an ice cream parlor selling old-
fashioned ice creams. (Not open in winter.) The
second floor, known as the Hall, contains a wide
array of merchandise not available on the first floor.

BRIAR LANE JAMS & JELLIES
230 Briar Ln, Wellfleet, 561-632-1122
www.briarlane.com
Roadside stand open from Memorial Day to
Columbus Day 10-6 daily except Wednesday, when
they are closed.
They've been making and selling jams and jellies at
this stand since 1932, and they say they use the same
recipes now as they did then. Really gorgeous gift
baskets of jam and jellies. 45 different jams, jellies,
marmalades. (They use pure cane sugar, not corn
syrup.) Marmalades made from cranberry, lemon
ginger, orange or peach. Some really different jams
and jellies: jalapeno, rhubarb, gingered pear, spiced
cranberry and dozens more.

BROWN JUG

155 Main St, Sandwich, 508-888-4669

www.thebrownjug.com

Open all year (usually 10-6), but with shortened hours Jan-Apr.

What started out as a gourmet grocery in 2003 has grown to include a very nice cafe serving beer and wine (indoor or outside in the summer). The store is still the main focus: cheeses, wines, foie gras, gift baskets. Great place to pick up the ingredients you'll need for a nice picnic.

CANDY MANOR
484 Main St, Chatham, 508-945-0825
www.candymanor.com
Handmade chocolates by the same family since 1955.
Definitely worth a swing by: hand dipped chocolates
are a big surprise, chocolate truffles, turtles, creams,
clusters, caramels. The homemade fudge comes in a
dizzying array of flavors: chocolate Oreo, walnut,
mint, raspberry, cappuccino, peanut butter, many
others.

CHRISTINA'S JEWELRY
www.christinasprovincetown.com
Open since 1982, this has been a one-stop destination
for all your jewelry needs. Now shopping is available
online only. You'll find handmade creations created
by well-known designers such as Ed Levin, Janice

Girardi, and Chris Bales. Also diamond rings, wedding bands, gemstone jewelry, and genuine beach glass creations by local artisans. The gift department features items that include mirrors, jewelry boxes, and Tiffany-style stained-glass windows.

DESIGN WORKS
159 Rte 6A, Yarmouth Port, 508-362-9698
www.designworkscapecod.com
Two sisters run this operation (Ann Hill and Margaret Hill), offering a creative mix of antiques, glassware, gifts, clothing, furnishings, bed & table linens, tableware, jewelry. Great gift ideas.

FOREST BEACH DESIGNER GOLDSMITHS
436 Main St, Chatham, 508-945-7334
www.capecodcharms.com
This is a working studio offering a collection of hand-made jewelry – most made by the resident goldsmiths.

JOAN PETERS OF OSTERVILLE

885 Main St, Osterville, 508-428-3418

www.joanpeters.com

Joan's toile is seen on lots of things in this store located in a charming cottage. Sea shell toile, Nantucket toile, Boston toile, Cape Cod toile, lots and lots of fabrics, baskets, limited edition fabrics and wallpapers, custom carpets, lots more.

MAP

188 Commercial St, Provincetown, 508-487-4900

No website.

Sells clothes and gifts, books, odd jewelry, necklaces, belts, housewares. Attracts a very interesting crowd. (You'll see what I mean when you go in here.)

MARION'S PIE SHOP
2022 Main St, Chatham, 508-432-9439
www.marionspieshopofchatham.com
Specializes in just that—homemade pies. Dutch
Apple, Wild Blueberry, Blueberry Crumb, Cranberry
Apple, Cran Peach Praline, Cherry, Baileyberry,
Bumbleberry, Blackberry, Blueberry Peach, Boston
Cream, Chocolate Cream, Lemon Meringue,
Raspberry, Razzleberry, Strawberry Peach,
Strawberry Rhubarb—that's just a few of them. Lots
of breakfast foods as well: coffee cake, cinnamon bun
rolls, blueberry muffins. Also has a long list of
specialty comfort foods: Meatballs, Tomato Sauce,
Stuffed Peppers, Eggplant Parmesan, Chicken
Parmesan, Shepherd's Pie, Macaroni & Cheese,
Seafood Casserole, Lobster Rolls, Garlic Bread,
Boston Baked Beans, Potato Salad, Cole Slaw, Pasta
Salad, Chicken Salad, Crab Cakes, Bacon, Broccoli,

or Spinach Quiche, New England Clam Chowder
Base, Mashed Potato, Chili, Portuguese Kale, Tomato
Cheddar, Bread Pudding, Ice Cream, Coffee, Tea and
Nantucket Juices.

MIDSUMMER NIGHTS
THE CHATHAM HOME
443 Main St, Chatham, 508-945-5562
www.thechathamhome.com
Owners Sarah Rhinesmith Buckley and Missy Smith
have a very original collection of items in the old ship
captain's house they've converted into a store:
porcelain sea urchins, steel lanterns, women's
clothing, accessories, home furnishings, linens, great
things for the house, gifts.

NAUSET FARMS
199 Main St, Orleans, 508-255-2800
www.nausetfarms.com
NEIGHBORHOOD: Orleans
Butcher and fish market with deli service. Great
sandwiches, fresh ingredients, gluten-free options.

NORTHERN LIGHTS HAMMOCK SHOP
361c Commercial St, Provincetown, 727-344-6250
www.northernlightshammocks.com
Tiny little "shop in a shack" has everything you can
imagine with the word "hammock" attached:
hammock stands, swing stands, hammock swing
stand accessories, great totes, casual furniture, gongs
and chimes, massage and comfort chairs.

OUTER CAPE KITES
277-A Commercial St, Provincetown, 508-487-6133
No website.
We're talking kites. More kits than you can imagine.
The kids will love this place and, though you might
not think you will, wait till you get here.

PAINTED DAISIES
679 Old King's Hwy, East Sandwich, 508-375-0713
www.painteddaisies.com
A unique gift shop popular among locals and tourists
offering a beautiful selection of gifts, jewelry and
home décor items. Lots of examples of work from
local artisans and craftspeople.

PERIWINKLE
25 Bank St, Wellfleet, 508-349-7731
http://periwinklewellfleet.com
Located in a cozy house is this store with lots of great
things for home and garden. Dishes, swerving bowls,
glassware, interesting linens, towels. Great place for
gifts.

PROVINCETOWN BOOKSHOP
246 Commercial St, Provincetown, 508-487-0964
https://homeportpress.com
Filmmaker John Waters used to run this charming
bookstore when he was a young man. And hey, it's a
bookstore. Visit one while you can.

RING BROS. MARKETPLACE
485 Rte 134, South Dennis, 508-394-2244
www.ringbrosmarketplace.com

NEIGHBORHOOD: South Dennis
One stop market for nearly everything with shops like: Chatham Fish & Lobster, Dark Horse Beef & Deli, Harney's Wine & Liquors, Hissho Sushi, Montilio's Bakery, Nata's Noodles, Ring Bros Produce & Grocery, & Spinners Pizza & Burritos. This place even offers a full service floral department, a gift & housewares department and made-to-order fruit baskets.

SANDWICH ANTIQUES CENTER
131 Rte 6A, Sandwich, 508-833-3600
www.sandwichantiquescenter.com
Quite a few rooms to go through here. It may look like a packrat's paradise, but the prices don't reflect that. There are a lot of antique stores on the Cape, and you expect to pay more because you're here and not some backwater town in the western part of the state. But even if you don't buy, this is a great place to browse.

Copper   Brass   Green

Seeded glass   Optic glass   Clear glass   Extra Large

Available in: four sizes ● three finishes ● three glass choices

SANDWICH LANTERN
17 Jan Sebastian Dr, Sandwich, 508-833-0515
www.sandwichlantern.com

This shop offers handcrafted lanterns created locally. Lanterns are crafted of solid brass and solid copper, many of the designs date back to the 1800s. They also have multiple colored glass options, hand-blown at the **Sandwich Glass Studio** right here on Cape Cod.

SCARGO POTTERY & ART GALLERY
30 Dr Lord's Rd, Dennis, 508-385-3894
www.scargopottery.com
Original pottery creations by artists Kim Holl, Mary Peabody, Meden Parker, Sarah Holl and Tina Holl. Hundreds of items to look at; bowls, pitchers, cups, platters, sculpture. There's a lot of work out in the garden you can take a look at even when the shop is closed.

SHELL SHOP
276 Commercial St, Provincetown, 508-487-1763

www.theshellshop.com
Blown glass, jewelry, starfish, specimen shells, large decorator shells, coral.

THE SPOTTED COD
153 Main St, Sandwich, 508-888-8263
No website
A favorite of home designers, here you'll find beautiful gifts and design elements for your home including pillows, fabrics, dishes, and other decorative items.

THREE BUOYS (BUOYS ON MAIN)
546 Main St, Harwich Port, 774-408-7720
Creative gifts and accessories can be found here.

THE WEATHER STORE
146 Main St, Sandwich, 800-646-1203
www.theweatherstore.com
Now this is an interesting store. Carries everything weather-related: barometers, thermometers, tide clocks, weather glasses, hygrometers, barographs, rain gauges, compasses, a great selection of weathervanes, and a lot of antique versions of these instruments. Definitely a place to get a gift that will forever be a conversation starter.

WEEKEND
217 Main St, East Orleans, 508-255-9300
www.capeweekend.com
Can you think of a better name for a store? Mari Porcari used to be a set designer and in this store built in 1835 has collected an amazing selection of items:

handbags, jewelry, accessories, art by Cape Cod artists, gifts and clothes for babies and kids, fragrances and women's clothing.

WELLFLEET MARINE STORE
25 Holbrook Ave, Wellfleet, 508-214-0677
www.wellfleetmarine.com
Besides the 2 boatyards they run, as well as a fish market, they have a really nice gift shop, and that's why you want to come here. Distinctive dresses, shirts, pants, as well as Donna Credit's nautical map jewelry.

WEST BARNSTABLE TABLES
2454 Meetinghouse Way, West Barnstable, 508-362-2676
www.westbarnstabletables.com
A wonderful shop that showcases beautiful custom furniture. Yes, you can furnish your entire home here with unique pieces including tables, cabinets, and cupboards – all quality pieces. Some of the woods they use to fashion the tables and cupboards here are antique, though most of the wood is new. Custom orders available.

WHISPERING COWGIRL
10 Main St, Wellfleet, 508-214-0158
www.whisperingcowgirl.com
Leather was naturally interesting to someone who loved horses, but besides bridles and saddles, she ended up with this store offering offbeat "western" or "country" fashions with style.

WICKED THRIFT
416 Rte 28, W Dennis, 508-648-5902
533 Main St, W Yarmouth, 508-648-5902
www.wickedthrift.com
The stock here is gathered by trading with customers.
(It's not a consignment shop.) You'll find men's and
women's clothing, shoes, bags, accessories, jewelry.
A men's shop called Swanky Joe's has, well, swanky
things for the Joe in your life. The original shop was
in the barn, but it was enlarged when they moved into
the Victorian house.

INDEX

T

U

V

W

WOODS HOLE SCIENCE AQUARIUM, 120

YARMOUTH HOUSE, 101

Y

Z

YARDARM, 101

ZOE'S PIZZA, 102

Ingram Content Group UK Ltd.
Milton Keynes UK
UKHW021027140323
418553UK00015B/938